TWAYNE'S WORLD AUTHORS SERIES
A Survey of the World's Literature

GREECE

Theocritus

TWAS 609

THEOCRITUS

By STEVEN F. WALKER
Rutgers University

TWAYNE PUBLISHERS
A DIVISION OF G. K. HALL & CO., BOSTON

Published in 1980 by Twayne Publishers,
A Division of G. K. Hall & Co.
All Rights Reserved

Printed on permanent/durable acid-free paper and bound
in the United States of America

First Printing

Library of Congress Cataloging in Publication Data

Walker, Steven F.
Theocritus.

(Twayne's world authors series ; TWAS 609 :
Greece)
Bibliography: p. 159-63
Includes index.
1. Theocritus—Criticism and interpretation.
PA4444.W3   884'.01   80-15705
ISBN 0-8057-6451-8

For John H. Finley, Jr.

Contents

About the Author

    Preface

    Chronology

1. The World of Theocritus   13
2. The Seven *Pastoral Idylls*   34
3. The Other Poems   85
4. The Literary Background of the *Idylls*   113
5. The Influence of Theocritus   133
    Notes and References   151
    Selected Bibliography   159
    Index   164

About the Author

Steven F. Walker received his B.A. in Greek from the University of Wisconsin-Madison in 1965, and a Ph.D. in Comparative Literature in 1973 from Harvard University, where he was a teaching fellow from 1969 - 1971. He is presently an Associate Professor of Comparative Literature at Rutgers University. The author has published articles on English, French, Spanish and Sanskrit poetry in *PMLA, Studies in Philology, Kentucky Romance Quarterly, Literature East and West* and *The Explicator*.

Preface

The days are long gone when the pastoral poems of Theocritus could be appreciated—or dismissed—as simple pictures of country life. The modern reader is far more likely to see at work in them what Empson, in an oft-quoted definition of Pastoral, called a process of "putting the complex into the simple." It is also a sign of a new appreciation of the purely literary merit of the *Idylls* that modern Theocritean scholarship has increasingly turned to problems of interpretation, in recognition of the fact that only a sophisticated critical approach can do justice to poetry of this caliber.

In this study, the first book-length critical introduction to the works of Theocritus to appear in English, I have tried to convey to professional Hellenists and Greekless readers alike my own sense of the thematic complexity of Theocritus' poetry at its best, and to indicate some of the points of interpretation which have been raised in recent Theocritean scholarship. I have also proposed a reading of the *Pastoral Idylls* (*Idylls* I, III - VII, and XI) as a *poetic sequence*, a reading which should be of interest to aficionados of Theocritean Pastoral, but which also provides the student approaching the *Idylls* for the first time with a unified perspective on the seven most influential poems of the collection. For comparatists interested in the problem of the Theocritean roots of European Pastoral, I have given in the last chapter a brief account of the influence of Theocritus over the centuries.

My personal thanks go to Professor Janet Walker, who reviewed the manuscript in its final stages; to Professor Charles P. Segal (Brown University) and Professor Ralph Johnson (University of California at Berkeley), who gave most generously of their time and energy when an anxious young comparatist facing a tenure decision sent them a manuscript to evaluate at short notice, and helped someone they did not know as though he had been a colleague of many years standing (such good deeds ought not to be allowed to perish in silence!); to two former teachers, Robert Fitzgerald and the late Cedric Whitman, who combined grace of mind with scholarly precision, and who also took time out from personal concerns to read the manuscript; to Mrs. Helen Homiak, for her excellent typing; and, finally, to Professor John Finley, who introduced me to Theocritus many years ago, and then, like the Auvergnat in the song, gave the warmth of his encouragement when encouragement was needed; it is only fitting that this book should be dedicated to the one who provided the first inspiration.

A passage from Gavin Maxwell's *The Ten Pains of Death* (New York, 1960) has been quoted by permission of the publisher, E. P. Dutton and Co., Inc. The photograph of the Hellenistic Head of a Satyr, in which the reader may imagine the spirit of the Daphnis or Damoetas of *Idyll VI* to be imprisoned, is reproduced with the permission of the Art Museum, Princeton University, where the original is on display as part of the C. O. von Kienbusch, Jr., Memorial Collection; it may be dated as early as the time of Theocritus. Unless otherwise noted, all translations are my own.

Rutgers University, New Jersey

STEVEN F. WALKER

Chronology

B.C.

331   Foundation of Alexandria by Alexander the Great.

c. 310 - 300 Birth of Theocritus, probably in Syracuse.

285 - 247 Reign of Ptolemy Philadelphus.

c. 280 - 270 Composition of the *Pastoral Idylls* and other major poems.

c. 280 - 240 Golden Age of Alexandrian Literature.

270   Death of Epicurus.

212   Roman conquest of Syracuse; death of Archimedes.

CHAPTER 1

The World of Theocritus

GENERALLY speaking, we know very little about the lives of the Greek poets of antiquity. Although much biographical information (and misinformation) has survived about the lives of the political notables and philosophers of ancient Greece, we have at hand no Plutarch, no Diogenes Laertius to give us the details of the biographies of the Greek poets. In the case of Theocritus, a few sentences are all that remain of whatever biographical material may have once existed.[1]

But perhaps the loss is not of major importance. The words and deeds of statesmen and generals survive to shed glory or opprobrium on their names only if they are somehow preserved in the collective memory; their words and deeds are the material out of which biographies are fashioned in order to preserve what was most memorable in their lives for later generations. As for the lives of philosophers, it is a healthy instinct (although a rather repressed instinct in modern times) to wish to test a philosopher's ideas against the actual conduct of his life. Thus Socrates is still loved and admired as much for his life as for his logic. But the situation with poets may be said to be special. A poet's most important words and deeds survive if his poems survive. His poems *are* his most memorable words and deeds, as far as we are concerned; and our best knowledge of him as a poet coincides with our deepest understanding of his poems.

Fortunately, it is likely that most of the poetry of Theocritus has survived; thanks to the efforts of innumerable copyists, commentators, emendators, and editors, we know his most memorable words and deeds. Otherwise, we know little about him: a few dates more or less secure, give or take a year or a decade; the names of a few places associated with his presence; and the names of a few persons who apparently played a role in his life. His historical milieu, on the other hand, has been the object of much study of late, as historians

13

have turned their attention to the Hellenistic period, which opened
with the death of Alexander the Great in 323 B.C., and to the Golden
Age of Alexandrian Literature, which encompassed the years 280 -
240 B.C. approximately.[2] The problem remains to relate the poet's
work to his historical world; no other area of literary history is so full
of pitfalls and uncertainties. A certain amount of pure speculation
wil be necessary. It is impossible to write much on the life of
Theocritus, if by "life" is meant a factual biography. But we do
have a poetic work, and we do know some things about our poet's
world—all that remains to be done is to put the two together.

I   Syracuse and Sicily

The Greek city of Syracuse in Sicily could look back on over four
hundred years of history by the time Theocritus was born there
about the year 300 B.C.[3] Colonists from the city of Corinth in the
Peloponnesus had founded Syracuse in the second half of the eighth
century B.C., and had brought with them that Doric dialect of Greek
which was to become one of the distinctive features of the poetic
language of the *Idylls*. "So we speak with a Peloponnesian accent,"
says the indignant Syracusan lady in *Idyll XV* ll.92 - 93 whose accent has just been ridiculed by an Alexandrian; "we Dorians have
the right to speak Doric, don't we?" These Dorian colonists had
eliminated, displaced, or assimilated the original inhabitants of Sicily, the Sicels, and by 500 B.C. the eastern part of the island as far in-
land as Enna seems to have been Hellenized. Soon the Sicilian
Greeks had established the basis for the island's legendary wealth
from agriculture and stockbreeding. The latter occupation was especially associated with the slopes of Mt. Etna, an immense volcano
whose snowy summit loomed over the pasturelands, vineyards, and
farms of the Sicilian Greeks from its height of more than 3,200
meters. It was on the slopes of Mt. Etna that Theocritus placed the
cave of the mythical Cyclops Polyphemus who, secure in his
pastoral wealth of cheeses and cattle, drank the pure water of Etna's
snow-fed streams and gazed out to sea when, in *Idyll XI*, he cher-
ished an unrequited love for the sea nymph Galatea. Theocritus
calls this one-eyed creature "my compatriot" in *Idyll XI* l.7, and
presents him as an archetype of the Herdsman-Poet. But in the
ninth book of Homer's *Odyssey*, when Odysseus and his men are
imprisoned in the cave of Polyphemus and only escape by blinding
his one eye and by riding under the bellies of his sheep, the Cyclops

is a monster with a barbarous taste for human flesh. Such by the time of Theocritus was the reputation of Sicily before the Greek settlement!

The later story of Polyphemus and Galatea is a reminder to us that Greek Sicily, like most of the Greek world, was a landscape in which various spots were associated with local myths and legends. At Enna, for example, the traveler could gaze on those flowery fields whose pastoral tranquillity had once been shattered when Hades (Dis), divine ruler of the Underworld, burst the ground with a chariot drawn by four black horses, and carried Demeter's daughter Persephone (Proserpina) off to his infernal realm. In Book IV of *Paradise Lost*, Milton compared Eden with

> that faire field
> Of *Enna*, where *Proserpin* gathring flours
> Her self a fairer Floure by gloomie *Dis*
> Was gatherd. . . .

In the very heart of Syracuse, on the island of Ortygia, the fountain Arethusa flowed with the waters of the Peloponnesian homeland. According to the myth, the god of the river Alpheus in the Peloponnesus had pursued the nymph Arethusa under water from his own native shores to the very spot where she was transformed into a spring in whose waters his own were mingled. This fountain Arethusa symbolized the city of Syracuse, and the nymph often appeared on its coinage. Daphnis, that legendary herdsman-poet from the slopes of Mt. Etna, was to bid that fountain and its nymph a fond adieu in *Idyll I* l.117.

Sicily, and Syracuse in particular, could lay claim to some glory as the homeland of several distinguished literary figures; their works survive only in fragments. Stesichorus was active in Sicily in the middle of the sixth century B.C.; his lyric treatment of epic themes is not without some connection with *Idylls XIII* and *XXIV*, which deal with two episodes in the life of that greatest of all Greek heroes, Heracles. Epicharmus was hailed as "the one who invented Comedy" by Theocritus in his eighteenth epigram, which commemorated a statue erected by the Syracusans to honor their distinguished fifth-century comic poet. In the same century, Corax of Syracuse and his pupil Tisias founded the Greek art of rhetoric, and Gorgias of Leontini, a town between Syracuse and Mt. Etna, brought this new art to Athens in 427 B.C. Perhaps the most important writer to have had an influence on the *Idylls* of Theocritus was Sophron, a Syracusan whose mimes may have influenced Plato's dialogues as well.

The actual herdsmen of Sicily and their bucolic songs and singing contests·may have played their part in inspiring the pastoral idylls of Theocritus, as the following anecdote preserved by the scholiasts seems to indicate.[4] At some time or another Syracuse was afflicted either by a plague or (the facts are not clear) by that other plague of Greek city states, civil strife. The goddess Artemis was credited with bringing whatever misfortune it was to an end, and a festival was instituted in her honor. The custom was for the herdsmen of the surrounding region to leave their pastoral haunts, gather as a group in the municipal theater of Syracuse, and delight the city dwellers and the goddess with the unusual spectacle of a bucolic singing contest where herdsman vied with herdsman for the prize. The losers in this contest would leave the theater and go forth in groups called "bucoliasts," singing and shouting out into the suburbs, and giving the Syracusans, who lived in what was by the year 400 B.C. the largest and most fortified of all the Greek cities, a taste of country life and country music. It is certainly tempting to imagine Theocritus witnessing such spectacles as a child, and later looking back on his childhood and saying, like Wordsworth in *The Prelude* (*VIII* l.128): "Shepherds were the men that pleased me first."

By the time Theocritus was a small boy, Syracuse had grown used to the rule of dictatorial regimes whose successive periods of stability were linked by periods of civil strife, during which the Syracusans exercised their right to war between the classes, until a new strong man arrived on the scene to put them in their place as subjects, not as citizens. Plato made a visit to one of these tyrants, Dionysius I, in 387 B.C. A story told about him illustrates the danger of involving oneself too closely with a Syracusan tyrant's private life. A poet in Syracuse by the name of Philoxenus was on friendly terms of patronage with Dionysius, eating at his table, and so forth. Dionysius had a mistress whose name, or professional name, was Galatea, which will remind the reader of that nymph who was the object of the affections of the Cyclops Polyphemus of great Sicilian fame. When Philoxenus was caught in the act with Galatea, Dionysius withdrew his hospitality, and sent his court poet off to the stone quarries. In this dismal prison, perhaps the very spot where the captured Athenians of the ill-fated expedition to conquer Syracuse in 415 B.C. had been detained, Philoxenus wrote a poem about Polyphemus, Galatea, and Odysseus, in which the Syracusan tyrant appeared as the Cyclops, and the author himself as Odysseus. The role of Galatea, of course, required no change of name. Theocritus probably knew the story; in all events, it is typically Syracusan.

Plato's disenchantment with the son of Dionysius I is well known—Dionysius II had the makings of a tyrant, but not of a philosopher king. By the time of the birth of Theocritus, another tyrant by the name of Agathocles had seized control of the government, was ruling with the support of the working classes, and was reviving the prosperity of Syracuse. It is not clear what kind of family Theocritus was born into, but an epigram *(XXVII)* attributed to him, although probably by a later editor of his works, seems to indicate that his family was not a prominent one. This poet of common birth, if such he was, later made petition to a Syracusan tyrant of common birth, Hiero II, in *Idyll XVI*. It is sad to report that, according to the scholarly consensus, the petition, itself one of the better poems of Theocritus, met with no success. Was this the reason why Theocritus left Syracuse?

II   Cos

It is perhaps strange that Theocritus should be presumed to have left the wealthy metropolis of Syracuse for the small island of Cos off the coast of Asia Minor. One tradition assumes that he was simply on his way to Alexandria, where the patronage of Ptolemy Philadelphus had drawn him along with many other poets and men of letters. But Cos may well have been his final destination, and not merely a halt in his journey. Three speculative considerations will be entertained. First of all, Theocritus may have been Coan in descent, and since family and local ties were maintained as a rule between Greek emigrants and those who stayed behind, Theocritus probably had connections on the island of Cos. *Idyll VII* ("The Harvest Festival"), the main source among the poems of Theocritus for this hypothetical stay on Cos, shows our poet on good terms with the local landowning aristocracy. The idyll begins and ends as a description of a visit which Theocritus and two friends made to the farmlands of Phrasidamus and Antigenes, two Coans of noble descent, who were sponsoring a harvest festival.

The second consideration concerns the famous school of medicine on the island of Cos. Cos, the homeland of Hippocrates, was one of the three main centers of the cult of Asclepius, as famous for its medical research as for the religious cult itself. By the time we can imagine Theocritus on the island (the 270s B.C.), there existed outside of the city of Cos an Asclepieion, a sanctuary dedicated to the god of healing, Asclepius.[5] Its excavated ruins may be visited by the present-day tourist. At the time of Theocritus, the sanctuary and temple complex enjoyed great renown. One of the masterpieces of the fourth - century painter Apelles, the "Aphrodite rising from the foam," was on display at the sanctuary, which combined the attributes of an elegant health resort and a religiously oriented medical school. It is possibly this Asclepieion which Herondas describes in his fourth mime, a piece which has much in common with Theocritus' *Idyll XV* ("The Syracusan Women"), as we shall see in Chapter 4.

The writings of Theocritus make no mention of this Asclepieion, and we do not know for sure how closely he was associated with it, if at all. However, we do know that Nicias, one of the closest friends of Theocritus, was a physician, and that he may have studied at Cos. Theocritus addresses Nicias as a doctor in *Epigram VIII, Idyll XXVIII* ("The Distaff"), and in the opening of *Idyll XI*, a poem in which medical allusions are used to great effect. In addition, new evidence has been uncovered which suggests that Theocritus himself knew something of the type of medical science which was taught on Cos at the time of Nicias' training. In her article "Was Theocritus a Botanist?" Alice Lindsell has shown that the *Idylls* reveal an extraordinarily accurate knowledge of the plant life of the eastern Mediterranean: "Theocritus sings of eighty-seven different trees, shrubs, flowers, grasses and ferns. Practically all the references are in the *Pastoral Idylls*: that is to say, that in the small compass of about 1,200 lines he mentions nearly twice as many plants as Homer does in the whole *Iliad* and *Odyssey*."[6] Furthermore, these plants are frequently wild plants whose names were unknown to most Greeks of the time. A plausible explanation for this unusual scientific interest in plants is that Theocritus must have studied botany, a new science established by Theophrastus in Athens a generation or two before Theocritus reached maturity. Since Greek medical studies would surely have included a careful study of plants, most of which were considered to have some medicinal value, Theocritus may have picked up his botanical expertise while studying with his Milesian friend Nicias on Cos. This possibility is made more plausible by the fact that Theocritus is familiar primarily with the plants of Greece and the Greek islands, Sicilian and Egyptian plants being conspicuously absent from his *Idylls*.[7]

A third speculative consideration concerns Philetas, a Coan poet of the generation before Theocritus, who is mentioned by name in *Idyll VII* l.40. Philetas had been the tutor of Ptolemy Philadelphus, and it is quite possible that this distinguished scholar-poet presided over an informally organized school of poets on the island. His connections with the court of his royal pupil at Alexandria as well as his own genius and erudition would have made him an appropriate mentor for a younger poet struggling for recognition and patronage. Regardless of the other reasons which may have brought Theocritus to Cos, it may have been his attachment to the school of Philetas which led him to prolong his stay on the island, where he came into his own as a poet under the influence of halcyon days, good company, youthful enthusiasm, and an inspiring teacher.

Lycidas in *Idyll VII* is the most fascinating figure that we can associate with this Coan period with certainty. In fact, the main subject of *Idyll VII* ("The Harvest Festival") is the meeting of Theocritus, alias Simichidas, with the goatherd poet Lycidas: "He was a goatherd, and nobody would have taken him for something else, since a goatherd is what he most clearly resembled" (*VII* ll.13 - 14). Leaving aside the question whether Lycidas was an actual friend of Theocritus, or a fictional creation, we still must ask whether Lycidas was in fact a goatherd—lines 13 - 14 protest too much! Lycidas sings a song (*VII* ll.52 - 89) which, he says, was "composed on the hill" (*VII* l.51), and taken at face value this expression seems to indicate that Lycidas was no more than a poetically inclined goatherd who amused himself in his leisure moments with elaborate songs about his love Ageanax. But Theocritus-Simichidas also composed *his* song (*VII* ll.96 - 127) while he stayed with his cattle "on the hills" (*VII* l.92), and it is much harder to take the formula at face value in the case of Theocritus, whom we can hardly imagine herding cattle on Cos. Lycidas and Simichidas both enjoy literary gossip and shop talk: Simichidas praises the poetry of Philetas and Sicelidas as greater than his own (competing with them would be like "a frog competing with cicadas"—the Greeks loved the sound of cicadas), although he does not deny that many people think he is the greatest singer alive; and Lycidas speaks out against poets who vainly struggle to emulate the greatness of Homer—a literary controversy of the time. Thus it seems possible to conclude that Lycidas in *Idyll VII* represents an older colleague of Theocritus who had sometimes disguised himself as a goatherd, and that Theocritus, in his banter about composing his song "on the hills," is simply playing along with him. In other words, both Lycidas and Theocritus-Simichidas in *Idyll VII* enjoy *pretending* that they are herdsmen-poets.

Perhaps this bucolic masquerade was a sort of literary game which the followers of Philetas on Cos indulged in frequently. Knowing what we do of the antics of the young French *Pléiade* poets gathered around the learned and jovial Dorat in sixteenth-century Paris, it is not hard to imagine the pupils of Philetas dressed up in goatskins, sallying forth into the countryside on their way to one festival or another, or simply on a lark of their own. They would stop now and then to improvise verses in good pastoral fashion—perhaps Theocritus had told them about the herdsmen and their songs at the Artemis festival in Syracuse. One day they must have admired the way in which Theocritus had transformed their carefree bucolic antics into the first outlines and yet unpolished fragments of what were to become his famous *Pastoral Idylls*.

Of course, it is equally possible that Lycidas was a strictly fictional creation, a literary reincarnation of the archetypal Herdsman-Poet whose mythic image fascinated Theocritus the way the story of the Scholar-Gypsy fascinated Matthew Arnold (see Chapter 2). However, there is something so idiosyncratic, so startlingly vivid in the figure of Lycidas as he appears in *Idyll VII* that one can easily imagine the meeting between him and Theocritus-Simichidas as the poetic transformation of an actual event. I am most reminded in this context of a painting by Courbet which also produces the effect of an actual moment preserved by some miracle from the sweep of time. In this painting (*The Meeting*, 1854), the painter shows himself and a wealthy patron being introduced to each other in a bright but nondescript part of the pastoral countryside of southern France. Dressed in simple workingman's clothes, staff in hand, the painter tilts his head and black, pointed beard upwards in a gesture of jaunty self-assertion and pride, while his wealthy and elegantly dressed patron stands hat in hand to greet the genius with proper humility. In the figure of Lycidas we have this same combination of humble appearance and artistic pride; like the figure of Courbet, Lycidas seems to relish the ironic contrast.

It remains to be seen why this bucolic masquerade might have had such an appeal for Theocritus and the Coan circle. In the case of Courbet's painting, we know that the jaunty stance of the Worker-Painter translated a political position: the working man, not the idle man of wealth, deserves the greater respect in society. Courbet's socialist politics are well known; but in the case of Theocritus, where no such knowledge exists, we are at a loss. Why would scholarly poets wish to disguise themselves as herdsmen, the lowest men on the Greek social totem pole? One theory, that of Reitzenstein, saw in the Theocritean bucolic masquerade a description of the Coan circle's ritual activity, with ceremonies related to the rites of Dionysus.[8] I prefer to see it as a sophisticated game, a playful manifestation of high spirits. But however playful the initial impulse (which in the Greek context especially does not preclude ritualistic elements), the game had a meaning to it. Perhaps the best place to begin the search for this meaning is with a look at some of the philosophical trends of the times.

III   *Diogenes and Epicurus*

By the time Theocritus can be imagined on Cos, the life of the Greek Cynic philosopher Diogenes (*c.* 400 - *c.* 325 B.C.) was already a legend.[9] Diogenes had given up everything in his youth for philosophy. But although moderation was preached and practiced by many philosophers, Diogenes carried the pursuit of the simple life to an extreme. In fact, he simplified his life in Athens so much that he was looked upon by many Athenians as little more than a hobo. He made his home in a cistern, sat down to eat in the marketplace out of a pouch in which he carried his food, and lived his life with absolutely no sense of shame or concern for privacy. Countless anecdotes existed about this eccentric philosopher who lived like a bum in the middle of the most civilized city of Greece. Nevertheless, his life-style was also seen as a perfect demonstration of *autarkeia,* of philosophical and practical self-sufficiency. His wisdom, his scorn of convention, and his physical endurance made him into a figure of charismatic appeal for many of the philosophically inclined Greeks of his time, and his legend spread rapidly throughout the Greek-speaking world.

What interests us here is the analogy between the legendary life of Diogenes, and the bucolic masquerade which we find in the figure of Lycidas in *Idyll VII* and elsewhere in the pastoral idylls of Theocritus. Diogenes looks and lives like a bum, but he is in fact a philosopher; Lycidas looks exactly like a goatherd, but in fact he is a poet. In both cases an extremely *ironic* persona is presented: Philosophy in rags, Poetry in goatskins. This is not to argue that Theocritus was a follower of the Cynic school of philosophy, but only to indicate that a model existed already for that ironic transformation of poet into goatherd which we have examined in *Idyll VII*.

Another philosopher, Epicurus, has recently been considered in connection with Theocritus and his *Pastoral Idylls*.[10] Epicurus (341 - 270 B.C.) was alive and still teaching in Athens at the time of Theocritus' stay on Cos. His particular life-style, as well as some of his ideas, may be seen dimly reflected in the *Pastoral Idylls*.

A concrete symbol of the Epicurean way of life was the well-known garden in Athens in whose delicate shade Epicurus gathered together his disciples for philosophical discussions. Unlike other philosophers who made their teachings directly available to all and sundry, Epicurus chose to withdraw from the social and political hubbub of Athens, and encouraged his followers to do likewise. Far from the madding crowd, the garden allowed him to lead a quiet life in the company of a select group of friends which included—this was unusual for the times—women and slaves as well as freemen. This garden thus became the symbol of the withdrawal from society *(ekchōrēsis)* of the Epicurean circle. It was so highly valued by Epicurus that he provided in his final will for its maintenance after his death for the benefit of his friends and disciples.

The "common life in the garden" of Epicurus and his friends presents obvious analogies with the bucolic life of the herdsmen-poets of the *Pastoral Idylls*. In the one case, we find friends discussing philosophy together in a garden; in the other, poets making poetry and discussing poetry together in some pleasant pastoral spot or *locus amoenus*. In addition, the presence of slaves and women philosophizing in the garden of Epicurus is as surprising as the presence of poetically gifted herdsmen in the *locus amoenus:* in ancient Greece, these three groups were usually denied access to higher culture. No doubt, the actual status of goatherds was hardly affected by the popularity of the *Pastoral Idylls!* Literature rarely has much direct influence on life, unfortunately. For the dispossessed of ancient Greece to have attained the rights and privileges of the leisured classes would have required a social revolution which was probably impossible given the economic realities of the times. The Epicurean circle can be appreciated as a small Utopian community nearly totally divorced from these economic and social realities; but outside of this charmed circle, we know, women and slaves were seldom allowed to give themselves over to the leisure of the philosophical life. In the same spirit, we can appreciate the pastoral vision of Theocritus in part as a Utopian vision which, for all its irony, presents an imaginary world where poets and herdsmen, the leisured and the dispossessed, have merged their formerly distinct styles of life in one unusual and unprecedented shared existence. The classless society of Theocritus' pastoral world breathes the spirit of Epicureanism.

Epicurus was convinced of the values of friendship: "of all the means which are procured by wisdom to ensure happiness throughout the whole of life, by far the most important is the acquisition of friends."[11] Greek culture traditionally valued friendship, much as modern Western society later exalted the value of romantic love. What was unusual in Epicurean philosophy and practice was the dissociation of friendship from the broader social and political concerns of the community.

The poetry of Theocritus is permeated with this new Epicurean ideal of friends living withdrawn from the larger community and sharing life's joys and sorrows together as a small group of kindred spirits. Indeed, the *Idylls* are the finest literary monument to friendship as it was felt and understood by the Epicureans. The word "friendliness" is a key to the emotional tone of much of the poetry of Theocritus. At times the expression of this friendly spirit is primarily sentimental, as when Corydon pulls the thorn out of Battus' foot in *Idyll IV* ll.50 - 57; at other times it rises to heights of enthusiasm and, free from all competitive spirit, rejoices at the fine poetry which a friend has created, as at the end of *Idyll I*.

The attitude of Epicurus toward sexual love was a very cautious one: "no one was ever the better for sexual indulgence, and it is well if he be not the worse."[12] Diogenes Laertius reports that "the Epicureans do not suffer a wise man to fall in love; . . . according to them love does not come by divine inspiration."[13] Their attitude was consistent with the Epicurean pursuit of pleasure, since pleasurable experiences which brought greater pain in their wake were to be avoided; for them, falling in love was mainly an occasion for painful disturbances of the mind and body. *Ataraxia*, freedom from painful disturbances, was the ideal.

Theocritus, if we can trust the evidence of his poetry, tended toward a certain amount of Epicureanism in his attitude toward sexual love. "Only poetry can cure love," he says to his friend Nicias at the opening of *Idyll XI;* and the rest of the poem demonstrates how poetry enabled the young Cyclops Polyphemus to rid his mind of an overwhelming passion for Galatea. In *Idyll VII*, Theocritus advises his friend Aratus to forget his passionate feelings for the reluctant Philinus: "let us make *hasychia* our chief concern." (*VII* l.126) *Hasychia*[14] can be taken as a poetic synonym for *ataraxia*; it indicates the peaceful existence and serene, cheerful outlook which accompany a life free from painful disturbances. And yet Theocritus, Epicurean as he so often seems in the *Pastoral Idylls*, was quite capable of describing the pathos and intensity of passion in other poems (*Idylls II* and *XIII*, for example), where the Alexandrian fascination with strong emotions guided him as a poet.

IV   *Alexandria*

In *Idyll VII* l.93 Theocritus-Simichidas claims that the fame of his songs may have reached the very throne of Zeus. Commentators on this line generally agree that Theocritus must have meant that Ptolemy II Philadelphus, the Macedonian lord of Egypt, had been impressed with the pastoral poetry of Theocritus, and was ready to show his appreciation of this literary achievement with active patronage. The road to royal patronage would naturally have led Theocritus to Alexandria, where Ptolemy rewarded poets with his favor. We have two indications that Theocritus' second journey across the sea was worth the time and trouble. *Idyll XVII* ("Encomium for Ptolemy"), although it can remind the reader of Theocritus' unsuccessful bid for the patronage of Hiero II in *Idyll XVI*, seems to be less a plea for help than an acknowledgment of patronage received. *Idyll XIV* ("Aeschinas and Thyonichus") is loud in its praise of Ptolemy: he is "benevolent, and cultured . . . a true king in his generosity" (*XIV* ll.61 - 64). The scholarly consensus is that Theocritus found in Alexandria the patronage he had sought in vain back in his native Syracuse.

"No lands produce so much as the flatlands of Egypt" (*Idyll XVII* l.79). The agricultural wealth of the valley of the Nile had been the basis of Egyptian splendor under the Pharaohs, and it continued to guarantee the prosperity of the new capital city of Egypt, Alexandria.[15] Alexander the Great founded this city on a nearly deserted stretch of the northwest coast of the Nile delta in 331 B.C., shortly after his conquest of Egypt. After the death of Alexander, his generals fought over the vast empire he had won for himself and the Greek-speaking world, an empire which stretched from the shores of the Adriatic to the valley of the Indus River. The empire was divided up, and Ptolemy I, the father of Ptolemy II Philadelphus, held on to Egypt as the heartland of his share of the empire and placed the body of the deified Alexander in a gold sarcophagus in the royal quarter of Alexandria. Greek-speaking immigrants poured in to help Ptolemy rule Egypt, and found in this recent conquest of the Macedonians a land of golden opportunities. Administrators as well as mercenary soldiers were needed in large numbers; tradesmen and artisans followed in their wake; and poets long used to going hungry found that it paid well to sing the praises of Ptolemy.

It is likely that Theocritus spent some time in Alexandria during the reign of Ptolemy II Philadelphus (285 - 246 B.C.). He would have found in this Greek city on the Mediterranean coast of Egypt a metropolis to rival his native Syracuse. Like Syracuse, Alexandria was a port sheltered by an island. Just as the fountain Arethusa on the island of Ortygia symbolized Syracuse, so Alexandria was known throughout the Greek-speaking world for the towering lighthouse which stood on the rocky tip of the island of Pharos which gave to it its name. The Pharos was completed about 280 B.C.; this techno-logical wonder of the age was a symbol of Alexandria's supremacy among Greek cities as well as of its orientation toward the Mediterranean sea routes and the Greek homeland which had sent so many of its people to this outpost of Greek civilization.

The streets of Alexandria teemed with newly arrived Greeks who had come to seek their fortune, among them no doubt the pro-totypes of the Syracusan ladies of *Idyll XV*. In this urban mime, two middle-class women, married and rather unaccustomed to the street life of Alexandria, make their way through the crowd toward the royal palace, where they hope to attend a concert in honor of Adonis. Their opinion of the native Egyptian population, the heirs to a civilization far more ancient than that of Greece, is none too high:

> Ye gods, what a mob! How will we ever manage
> to get through this invasion of swarming ants?
> Well, Ptolemy, you've done a lot of good things
> since your father became immortal: criminals
> don't mug you in the streets anymore

in the good old Egyptian tradition—they're all alike,
those devils with their dirty tricks!
(*Idyll XV* ll.44 - 48, 50)

This passage in *Idyll XV*, one of the few remaining Greek texts
where Egyptians are even mentioned in the early years of the
Ptolemaic empire, seems to confirm the hypothesis of Fraser, who
writes: "Very little is heard of the Egyptian population until the
end of the third century, and from this general silence we may infer
that the gulf between Greek and Egyptian was almost complete in
normal social intercourse of the middle and upper classes. . . ."[16]
The Greeks of this period ruled Egypt much as the British were
later to rule India.

Nevertheless, their ruler Ptolemy could hardly afford to alienate
the Egyptian priesthood, or fail to win the allegiance of the millions
of agricultural workers whose taxes paid for the splendors of the
Ptolemaic court and maintained the Greeks of Alexandria in relative
affluence. Shortly before Theocritus may be presumed to have
arrived in Egypt in search of patronage, Ptolemy Philadelphus
renounced his first wife and married his sister Arsinoe II (*c.* 276 - 75
B.C.), thus following the Egyptian custom according to which the
Pharaoh and his sister formed a divine royal couple. This submis-
sion to the dictates of Egyptian tradition, however politically astute,
was not necessarily appreciated by all the Greeks in Ptolemy's
kingdom. History has recorded the fate of one Greek who dared to
raise an objection: the poet Sotades, whose satirical verses on the
subject of brother-sister marriage went a bit too far, found himself
first in prison and then, after he had tried to escape, at the bottom
of the sea inside a leaden chest.[17] Theocritus was perhaps reminded
of the fate of the Syracusan poet Philoxenus, and resolved to say
nothing but good about Ptolemy.

The truth was that Ptolemy Philadelphus deserved a good deal of
praise. The royal quarter of Alexandria, an area which included gar-
dens, shrines, and public buildings as well as the palace complex,
was famous for two institutions which by themselves would have
sufficed to earn Ptolemy the undying gratitude of the Greek world:
the Museum and the Library.[18] The Museum (*Mouseion*) was, as its
name indicates, dedicated to the service of the Muses—we would
call it a research institute for the arts and sciences—and its library
was the prototype of all modern libraries.

We have no proof that Theocritus was at any time an associate of the Museum. But he probably received some form of royal patronage from Ptolemy Philadelphus, and the Museum symbolized more than anything else that generous and long-term patronage of the arts and sciences which made Alexandria the leading cultural center of the Greek world during his lifetime. Within the precincts of the Museum gathered some of the finest creative, scholarly, and scientific minds of Greece. It should be noted that the Coan contingent was one of the most important; Philetas of Cos had been the first eminent name associated with the court of the Ptolemies; and the Coan school of medicine was to remain the pool from which Alexandrian medical talent would be drawn for years to come.[19] Not only would Theocritus have found friends and professional colleagues from Cos in Alexandria, but also a young man from Syracuse, Archimedes, who was studying there at the time. Archimedes was later to enjoy as lasting a reputation as a mathematician and engineer as his fellow Syracusan Theocritus as a poet; like Theocritus, Archimedes used Syracusan Doric in his writings. Euclid, another mathematician whose name is known to every high-school student in the world today, was probably still alive and teaching in Alexandria at this time; his *Elements* have continued to provide the basis for the study of plane geometry in our own time. Aristarchus, another genius of the age, was astounding the scientific community with his theory of a heliocentric universe. While Theocritus and others were reviving the art of writing poetry in Greek, Greek science and mathematics were flourishing in Alexandria.

The poets and scholars who came and received royal stipends or the equivalent support from the generous hands of Ptolemy Philadelphus must have found the Library another good reason for prolonging their stay in Alexandria, in spite of the homesickness which grew as the projected return to their native cities was delayed time and again. In the third century B.C. it may have contained as many as several hundred thousand volumes. Demetrius of Phalerum, a pupil of Theophrastus but later exiled from Athens, started the collection in the reign of Ptolemy I Soter. By the time of Theocritus a generation of scholars had been making headway at the overwhelming task of collecting, cataloguing and editing the texts in which about five centuries of Greek literature and learning were preserved. The Alexandrian scholar-poets were not only concerned with preserving the vast legacy of Greek myths and literature, but also with giving these myths a new lease on on life in their poetry and reviving old literary forms whenever possible. As we shall see in Chapter 4, a certain amount of Theocritus' poetry reflects the concerns of the scholar-poets of Alexandria and the other international centers of culture of the age. Once we look beyond the *Pastoral Idylls*, we can easily maintain that one side of the genius of Theocritus was "Alexandrian" in the more restrictive sense of the term, and that the Museum and the Library probably played their part in guiding his poetic inspiration along less untrodden paths.

Alexandria at its height was more than a city, it was the most typical and outstanding creation of a new phase of Greek civilization. The modern Greek poet Cavafy, who lived 2,200 years after Theocritus in an Alexandria changed almost beyond recognition, was to look back with nostalgia on the city of the Golden Age of Alexandrian literature, and put the following words in the mouth of one of the early Ptolemies: "My city's the greatest preceptor, queen of the Greek world, genius of all knowledge, of every art" ("The Glory of the Ptolemies").[20]

V   *The Poet of the* Oikoumenē

In the vast empire which Alexander left to his successors after his death in 323 B.C., Greek culture reigned supreme. Before Alexander, the Greek homeland and its far-flung settlements on the shores of the Mediterranean were surrounded by more powerful or more primitive peoples who threatened the unstable peace which occurred whenever Greek city states were able to refrain from fighting among themselves. After Alexander, most Greek city states (but *not* Syracuse) had lost that autonomy and freedom of action which had frequently expressed itself at the expense of their neighboring city states; and the known inhabited world, as far as most Greek minds could imagine it extending, had paid homage to the armies of Alexander and to the Greek culture and language which came with them. For a brief moment, before Rome had clearly announced its presence on the stage of Mediterranean history toward the end of the third century B.C., the known inhabited world, *oikoumenē* in Greek, seemed to coincide with the Greek world and its spheres of cultural influence.

This *oikoumenē* was, of course, as much a state of mind as a political or cultural entity. For example, millions of Egyptians continued to live as they had always lived, with Ptolemy as their

Macedonian Pharaoh. But we have seen that, for the Greeks of Egypt, these Egyptians did not really count. Perhaps the best way to explain this new Greek state of mind is to contrast it with another and earlier one. The Greek reader of Xenophon's *Anabasis,* which described events taking place in the years 401 - 399 B.C., no doubt shuddered to realize how terribly lost a contingent of Greek mercenary soldiers could get, deep into hostile barbarian territory (barbarian = non-Greek), and thrilled at the account of the courage and resourcefulness it took for this small band of heroes to make their way back to the outposts of their own civilization. But seventy-five years later the world of the barbarians, once so frightening and alien, had become part of a Macedonian empire in which Greek culture and the Greek language (the Attic Greek which Philip II of Macedon had made the official language of his chancery earlier in the century) reigned supreme; the Persian Empire was no more, and Alexander's general Ptolemy was satrap of Egypt. The Greeks were now at home, more or less, in most of the known inhabited world, which was now *their oikoumenē.*

But there were dangers in this new cultural hegemony of the Greeks. Greek culture had been traditionally rooted in the life of the *polis,* the individual city state with its social institutions, political life, and history. The Greek settlements usually looked back with pride to the mother city which had founded them. "We are Syracusans, Corinthians by descent," the Syracusan ladies of *Idyll XV* reply heatedly to the Alexandrian who has criticized their Doric accent. In fact, they were also Alexandrians, cohabitants of a newly founded city, a city without roots, an open city where all Greeks were exiles from the city states they had left behind when they came to seek their fortune in Ptolemaic Egypt. The *oikoumenē* was full of such newly founded Greek cities, of which Alexandria-in-Egypt was only the most prominent; all over the *oikoumenē* the Greeks had made their homes, and lost their roots.

In his essay *De Exilio,* Plutarch deals with the problem of consoling someone who has been forced to leave his homeland. He points to the example of Demetrius of Phalerum, whose exile from Athens gave him the opportunity to begin the collection of the great Library in Alexandria, and says encouragingly: "Every city at once becomes a native city to the man who has learned to make use of it and has roots which can live and thrive everywhere and take hold in any region."[21] No doubt Theocritus and his fellow poets in Alexandria encouraged each other with similar exhortations, all the more

since, like most Greeks in the recently conquered areas of the
oikoumenē, theirs had been a voluntary exile. In addition, poets
were traditionally used to seeking out sources of patronage in far
away places. But for so many Greeks to be cut off from local roots in
the *poleis* at one time, thanks to the unbelievably quick progress of
Alexander's armies, which opened up so many lands of opportunity
for Greeks of all walks of life, must have created a tremendous feeling of collective malaise.

A new myth with the traditional therapeutic force which the
older myths had had in their time was needed by these Greeks who
lived in a state of permanent exile in the new cities of the
oikoumenē, and who, like Diogenes, could call themselves, not
citizens of one traditional polis or another, but *kosmopolitai*, World
Citizens. Theocritus created that myth. The new mythological in-
habitant of this new rootless world, the noble savage, the Universal
Man of the *oikoumenē*, is to be found in the figure of the
Herdsman-Poet as presented in the *Pastoral Idylls*. This figure, an
amalgam of the image of the cosmopolitan literatus who made his
career in the new centers of patronage with the image of the
traditional herdsman whose silhouette was an almost timeless
feature of the various landscapes of the *oikoumenē*, gave a sense of
rootedness to the sophisticated international culture of the Alexandrian age, and a sense of archaic simplicity to an age all too aware of
complexity.

The myth thus had a social function, but it is hard to define this
social function too precisely, given the little we actually know about
Greek society of the third century B.C. I will, however, suggest an
analogy. Just as the myth of the Tragic Hero created by the first
Athenian tragedians served to celebrate and justify the new weight
of individual dignity born in the democratic struggle against tyranny and to resolve the guilt of a radical break with the past, so the
Theocritean myth of the Herdsman-Poet celebrated and justified
the break which the Greeks of the *oikoumenē* had made with the
local traditions and culture of the *polis*, and encouraged them to
meet the challenge of their new rootlessness. It is as if Theocritus
had said something to this effect to his contemporaries: "You are
sophisticated Universal Men of the *oikoumenē*, and yet you belong
to the timeless pastoral landscape which surrounds the rootless cities
in which you live. Make the best of it; and, if you can, make
music." It is because Theocritus gave full expression to the new

myth of the age that he deserves to be called, in my opinion, the Poet of the *Oikoumenē*.

No doubt, all Greeks were not equally rootless in the age of Theocritus; for many, in the independent kingdom of Syracuse, for example, or in an Athens wrapped in the dream of her former glory, the force of local tradition and culture may have seemed as powerful as ever. Menander, the last great Athenian dramatist, refused to go to Alexandria; but his friend and fellow Athenian, Demetrius of Phalerum, was exiled and had no choice but to step boldly into the cultural arena of the new age and make the best of it.

Nor was the learned poetry of Theocritus for everyone, or to everyone's taste. The first and initially most encouraging audience for the *Pastoral Idylls* was no doubt those groups of poets and scholars who flourished at Cos, Alexandria, and the other new centers of Hellenistic culture and patronage. These literati, polished by centuries of Culture, socially democratic yet cut off by a scholarly sense of tradition from a popular audience's cosmopolitan vulgarity, could most readily catch an ironic glimpse of their way of life reflected in the *Pastoral Idylls*. But Ptolemy Philadelphus, we remember, also fell under the spell of the *Pastoral Idylls*, and after him, we can presume, a wider audience throughout the *oikoumenē*, including perhaps even housewives like those of *Idyll XV* who made such efforts to hear the Adonis song and transcend through poetry and music the limitations of their narrow existences.

However, it would be an error to think that Theocritus' Herdsman-Poet myth and the genre of the Pastoral Idyll which he made into its literary vehicle merely reflected, in microcosmic form, the spirit of the age. If this were so, the *Pastoral Idylls* could be seen as an entirely typical product of the Alexandrian age, whereas in fact they are in many ways highly *un*typical. Theocritus is much more the typically Alexandrian poet in his nonpastoral poems, which present more obvious affinities with the works of his contemporaries Callimachus, Apollonius, Herondas, et al. The pedantic preoccupations of the scholarly poets of his age find little place in the *Pastoral Idylls*, and Theocritus responded to his age's antiquarian interest in the revival of old forms with the creation of a new and unusual form. But there is no need to continue this topic, since Chapter 4 will explain Theocritus' complex relationship with his Alexandrian contemporaries in greater detail than is necessary at this juncture.

It is pertinent, however, to examine briefly the "significant silences" (to borrow the term of Pierre Macherey)[22] of the texts of the *Pastoral Idylls*, that is to say, what they fail to tell us about the world in which Theocritus lived. Of the splendor and generous patronage of the Hellenistic courts, so prominent in the "Encomium to Ptolemy" and *Idyll XIV* ("Aeschinas and Thyonichus"), there is hardly a word; this silence in itself is worthy of comment, since later Pastoral, starting with Virgil, frequently made the flattery of the rich and powerful a hallmark of the genre. The deification of Alexander and his successors, the emotionalism of so much of Alexandrian literature and art, finds no response in Theocritus' pastoral vision, apolitical and Epicurean in its primary inspiration. The great cosmopolitan metropolis, the typical creation of the Hellenistic age, finds no reflection in the bright landscape and shady *locus amoenus* of the *Pastoral Idylls*, whose herdsmen inhabit the image of an earlier, simpler age. The small but complete world of the *Pastoral Idylls* resists what, after Leo Marx,[23] we could call the "counterforce" of the *oikoumenē*, the inhuman scale of its power and organization, the multitude and variety of the peoples who crowded into its shelter and under its banners. It was as though the spectacle of the magnificent achievements of the Macedonian monarchs left Theocritus indifferent. It was not that Pastoral was generically unable to sing the glories of empire; Virgil's *Eclogues* prove the contrary. It was simply that through the significant silences of his pastoral texts Theocritus was willing to consign major features of his age to oblivion. His pastoral vision is as remarkable for what it leaves out as for what it includes; it was a process of deliberate selection and rejection, not of simplification for its own sake.

In this presentation of Theocritus and his world, we must be content with considering some of the possible relations between the poet's work and the historical period in which he lived. The man himself has left few traces of his life; at best, we have been able to offer the reader a "group portrait, with poet" in which the poet's own features have been hopelessly blurred by the passage of time. But now it is time to take encouragement from the example of Albrecht Dürer. The German artist, after having engraved the following words in the upper lefthand corner of his magnificent portrait of Erasmus: "*Imago Erasmi Roterodami ab Alberto Durero ad vivam effigiem deliniata*" (This is the likeness of Erasmus of Rotterdam, sketched from life by Albrecht Dürer), added the following words in Greek below them, almost as an apology: *"tēn kreittō ta syngrammata deixei"* (but his own writings will reveal his likeness to you better).

CHAPTER 2

The Seven Pastoral Idylls

THE pastoral corpus of Theocritus consists primarily of the seven idylls numbered *I, III, IV, V, VI, VII*, and *XI*. Although the reader will find other idylls sometimes referred to as pastoral in discussions of Theocritus, I have not included them in this list, either because they are probably not by Theocritus (*Idylls VIII* and *IX*), or because the figure of the Herdsman-Poet, the hallmark of the genre, does not appear in them (*Idylls II, X*, and *XIV*).

There is another reason for restricting this chapter to a discussion of the seven *Pastoral Idylls*. It is my feeling that, read in the order given above, these poems form a poetic sequence. Gilbert Lawall, in his book *Theocritus' Coan Pastorals* (1967), first proposed that *Idylls I - VII* be considered as an organized unity, as a "poetry book"; this hypothesis has since run into a lot of criticism.[1] In my opinion, Lawall's basic intuition was a fruitful one, since it called attention to the unity of Theocritus' pastoral vision in poems which at first might seem to present only a pleasing variety of themes and perspectives. However, I disagree with Lawall about the choice of the idylls which could constitute a unified collection. This more controversial aspect of my presentation of the *Pastoral Idylls* will be taken up in section VIII of this chapter.

I   Idyll I (*"Thyrsis"* or *"The Song"*)

Idyll I concerns a song which Thyrsis, a shepherd, sings for the benefit of his unnamed goatherd friend. The poem has two parts. The first is a narrative frame (ll.1 - 63, 143 - 52) which takes the form of a cheerful conversation between Thyrsis and the goatherd and includes an unusually detailed description of the scenes carved on a wooden cup (27 - 60). The conversation frames the song of Thyrsis (ll.64 - 145), which deals with the last moments of the dying cowherd archpoet Daphnis.

The poem opens with an evocation of the musical whispering *(psithurisma)* of the wind in the pinetree, to which Thyrsis compares the sweet sounds of the goatherd's music on the syrinx or panpipes. The word *hadu* ("pleasant," "sweet"), repeated first in reference to the whispering of the pinetree and then in reference to the goatherd's piping, establishes a correspondence between the pastoral landscape and the goatherd's music. The god Pan, inventor of the original panpipes or syrinx (the nymph Syrinx, pursued by Pan, underwent a sudden metamorphosis into the reeds which Pan then cut for his musical pipes), is also brought into the picture: "You will carry off the second prize, after Pan gets the first," says Thyrsis in line 3. Thus the goatherd's simple pastoral musical art is associated with the natural music of the pastoral landscape (the sound of the wind in the pines) and the pastoral god Pan.

A significantly different description is given of the music of the shepherd Thyrsis in lines 7 - 11. It is not simple piping, but vocal music, song *(melos)*. It is associated with the sound of water (the stream which splashes from the rocks), in comparison with which it is not sweet but sweet*er (hadion)*; water was traditionally associated with the high art of poetry.[2] Thyrsis' singing is thus more than a primitive recreation of Nature's sounds, and it is associated, not with the nature god Pan, but with the Muses, who traditionally inspired the more sophisticated forms of art. In drawing this distinction between the rustic piping of the nameless goatherd and the song of the shepherd Thyrsis, Theocritus is defining the relation between his own sophisticated verse and the bucolic folk art which it purports to imitate.

The second exchange of conversation between Thyrsis and the goatherd (12 - 26) deals playfully with the goatherd's superstitious fear of piping at noon (Pan's siesta would be disturbed) and his willingness to reward the shepherd Thyrsis with gifts if he will sing for him; in a subtle way it marks the distinction between his simple folk art and the more sophisticated art of Thyrsis' bucolic Muse (20). The goatherd wishes the shepherd to sing the song about the sufferings of the legendary cowherd archpoet Daphnis *(ta Daphnidos algea)*, the originator of pastoral verse and the archetype of all herdsmen-poets. It is clear that in this section of *Idyll I* Theocritus is intent on defining a hierarchy of pastoral art forms, from simple piping to that recreation of ancient myth and legend which was one of the preoccupations of Alexandrian poetry.

The second exchange leads without transition to a long and symbolically fascinating description of a wooden cup which the goatherd promises Thyrsis as a reward for singing "The Sufferings of Daphnis." This cup is, significantly, an *objet d'art* which the goatherd did not make himself but bought from a sailor who accepted a goat and a large cheese in exchange: "Goatherds are astonished at the sight of it," says the goatherd, "and it will amaze you, too" (56). Critics have been amazed by it as well, and have struggled to understand what, if anything, could have prompted Theocritus to place such a long and elaborate description of a work of art *(ekphrasis)* at this point in *Idyll I*. The young Alexander Pope, in his "Discourse on Pastoral Poetry" (1709), showed no appreciation whatsoever of the latent symbology[3] of the carved scenes on the cup, and wrote that Theocritus "is apt to be too long in his descriptions, of which that of the cup in the first pastoral is a remarkable instance." Considered as mere description, the *ekphrasis* of lines 27 - 60 is certainly overdone, and slows down the dramatic movement of the idyll quite needlessly. However, it is by no means an overdone and overly long descriptive passage, but rather another step in the symbolic definition of Theocritus' pastoral vision. Just as the earlier exchanges between the goatherd and the shepherd distinguished Theocritus' sophisticated verse from its rustic counterpart, so this passage presents a symbolic image of the nature of Theocritus' new poetic genre.

There are three scenes carved on the wooden surface of the cup. In the first scene, a beautiful woman is being courted by two suitors at once; she is not about to make her choice quickly, and lets the two wear themselves out trying to find the right words to please her mind. In the second scene, an old fisherman is about to cast his net into the sea; he strains his muscles, and seems to have the strength of a younger man. In the third scene (45 - 54), a young boy is plaiting a cricket cage (crickets were kept as pets, since their chirping was much appreciated in Antiquity). He is enjoying what he is doing so much that he fails to see two foxes prowling around, ready to snatch away his lunch and eat the grapes of the vineyard he is supposed to be guarding.

The dialectical progression implicit in the three scenes seems clear: the boy plaiting the cricket cage combines the work of the old fisherman with the cult of beauty of the two suitors, but all on a higher level, the level of free artistic creativity. The boy's work is accomplished in a spirit of play, and his project to capture the delight of the cricket's voice is free from the strain and hardship of unrequited passion. He is not working hard for his livelihood (if anything, he is somewhat negligent of the vineyard and his breakfast), and he has not yet come to the age when hunting crickets will give way to courtship. The boy is living, at least momentarily, in a better world which does not know the pain of erotic frustration or the necessity of hard physical labor. The small, artfully woven cricket cage, with its rustic overlapping of rush and asphodel, is a symbol of the pastoral poem itself; and the sound, absent but anticipated, of the captive cricket suggests the voice of the poet, captured in the meshing of sound and rhythm of the verbal texture of the poem. The cup seems to say that in the creation of such a pastoral object (cricket cage as well as pastoral poem) lies a happiness that transcends the rewards of the hardships of passion (the two suitors) and of work (the sea-worn old man). The cup is the symbol of Theocritus' pastoral *ars poetica*, his poetic credo.

The goatherd's next remark caps his plea to hear Thyrsis sing: "You can't take your song with you to Hades, where all is forgotten." (*I* ll.62 - 63) The allusion is appropriately lugubrious, since "The Sufferings of Daphnis" ends with the silent descent of that bucolic hero to Hades. The reader will not have any problem appreciating the gloomy atmosphere of the song, which is only briefly lightened by the attempts at humor on the part of Priapus. But there are other problems of interpretation which are, as it were, built into the song, and which call for special attention.

The song which Thyrsis sings raises several questions directly, and several other questions indirectly; all are left unanswered, or half-answered. The first question is one that Thyrsis raises himself at the very opening of the song, just after his "signature" verse: "Where were you, when Daphnis was wasting away, where were you, Nymphs?" (66). The Nymphs, who were friends of Daphnis (141), ought to have been with him in his hour of deepest distress; since they were not, Thyrsis guesses that they may have been away on a journey to Thessaly (67), since Thessaly is a Greek land about as far away from Sicily and Mt. Etna as can be imagined.[4] However, this is no satisfactory explanation. *Why* were these Sicilian nymphs not present at the death bed of Daphnis, when the herdsmen of the area, his own cattle, a rural godling, and two major divinities made a point of coming to voice their concern over his tragic plight? This implied question is simply left hanging.

Hermes, the inventor of the lyre and a divine patron of herdsmen, comes down from the mountain pastures. He has guessed that

Daphnis must be suffering from the pangs of unrequited passion:
"Who is tormenting you? For whom, my dear friend, have you con-
ceived such a passion?" (78). For whom, indeed! for Daphnis makes
no answer. It seems that Theocritus has deliberately chosen to present us with a riddle. If the story of Daphnis had been well known
to the Greek audience of the time, all these questions left unanswered would have amounted to a rather inept attempt at
mystification or a none too subtle attempt at irony, since even the
main characters in the story as presented by Theocritus in *Idyll I
cannot* understand what is happening to Daphnis.

Priapus, the funny little phallic god whose statue faces Thyrsis as
he sings (21), has what we would probably call a Freudian explanation of Daphnis' problem (82 - 83, 85):

> "Poor Daphnis! Why are you wasting away? The girl
> is roaming past every spring and through every glade
> searching for you; but you are just neurotic *[duserōs]*."

I apologize for using the modern term "neurotic" for *duserōs*, but it
has proved to be a devilishly hard word to translate.[5] Just what
Priapus means by *duserōs* he makes clear with a Priapic comparison:

> "You used to be called 'Daphnis the Cowherd' but you
>   look like a goatherd now.
> A goatherd, when he sees the nanny-goats mounted,
> starts to weep because he was not born a billy goat;
> and you, when you see how the maidens are laughing,
> start to cry because you are not dancing with them."

But this comparison only thickens the plot: why is Daphnis avoiding
the attentions of the "girl" (*kōra* 82) who is searching for him, and
why instead is he so disturbed by the fact that he cannot join in the
dance of the laughing maidens (*tas parthenos* 90)? And who is the
girl, and who are the maidens? These questions have been at the
center of a recent scholarly controversy.[6]

One eminently reasonable solution was proposed by Charles
Segal: "The very *mystery* of Daphnis' end may be the most essential element in the poem."[7] Such an approach to the problem really
ought to bring the scholarly controversy to an end, since if
Theocritus was being deliberately obscure, it was no doubt in order
to heighten the sense of the mystery surrounding Daphnis' death,

and not to provide an occasion for scholarly detective work to answer the question "Who (or what) did in poor Daphnis?"

However, Theocritus is not merely being obscure in his references to the Daphnis story; he is deliberately raising questions, withholding answers and generally tantalizing the reader with pieces of a puzzle which never quite fit together. I would suggest that Theocritus is goading the reader toward the realization that the death of Daphnis involves issues which are difficult to understand, not because the facts alone are hard to ascertain, but also because the situation itself is a most unusual one, since it does not reflect the ordinary human being's range of experience of life. Daphnis, like Oedipus or Antigone, was of heroic stature, and however much the heroic agony illuminates the human condition, it cannot be said to reflect the usual and more trivial problems of ordinary existence.

There existed a Sicilian myth according to which Daphnis had made a vow of fidelity to a nymph who had fallen in love with him; a princess seduced Daphnis while he was drunk, and the outraged nymph blinded him for breaking his vow. Some scholars have felt that this myth provides us with enough detail to clarify the situation of Daphnis in *Idyll I*. Thus the "girl" who is searching for Daphnis would be the still passionate princess, and the "maidens" would be the nymphs from whose company Daphnis' sexual infidelity has permanently excluded him. One could add that it is natural that the phallic godling Priapus would see no point in Daphnis' attitude, which was to gawk hopelessly at the dancing nymphs, and stupidly neglect the charms of the passionate princess—from the Priapic perspective, it would be a case of sexual neurosis and sheer stupidity. The problem with this interpretation is that it leaves us ultimately as puzzled as Priapus: why was Daphnis such a neurotic fool? One has to assume, of course, that Daphnis was still in love with his angry nymph, but the reference in *Idyll I* is not to a nymph, but to many nymphs—why should these other nymphs be so important to him?

Another interpretation sees in Daphnis a hero of chastity along the lines of the Euripidean Hippolytus.[8] Daphnis, in other words, would rather die than give in to the desires of his frantic Phaedra (the girl who searches for him over hill and dale). This interpretation has the advantage of accounting for Daphnis' bitter resentment of the power of Aphrodite (100 - 13), but is otherwise rather fanciful. Why should such a martyr to the cause of chastity be such a hero to the herdsmen of the *Pastoral Idylls*, whose own attitudes

toward the sexual dimension of life are quite easygoing? Hippolytus
would have cut a rather ridiculous figure in the pastoral world of
Theocritus—exactly the figure, in fact, of Priapus' goatherd, who
feels like a martyr of chastity when he looks on the spectacle of his
rutting goats. And assuming that Daphnis is just such a figure, why
does the song of the sufferings of Daphnis inspire awe rather than
mirth?

The problem with both of the above lines of interpretation is that
they fail to look for a specifically *Theocritean* perspective on the
Daphnis legend as it appears in *Idyll I*. Both involve a recourse to
an external frame of reference, as though the key to the mysterious
sufferings of Daphnis were to be found in a traditional myth. In my
opinion, we must look to the pastoral corpus of Theocritus for the
key to the perspective which would bring the elements of the
Daphnis legend, as we find them scattered in *Idyll I*, into some
meaningful conjunction. Are there any helpful parallels in any of
the other pastoral idylls which can give us a clue as to the meaning
of Daphnis' death?

In *Idyll VII* another account of the death of Daphnis is given:
"Daphnis the cowherd was in love with Xenea, and the hillside
showed its concern and even the oaks on Himera's banks broke out
into lamentation, while he wasted away like melting snow . . ."
(*VII* ll.72 - 76). Apparently, as Hermes suspected, Daphnis had
been passionately'in love at some time or another. But this second
Theocritean version of the story still does nothing to explain if or
how Daphnis' love for Xenea, whoever she was, led to his sufferings
and death.

The most general interpretation that can be drawn from the account of Daphnis in both *Idylls I* and *VII*—and it is easily drawn,
without imagining details or connections where none are given—is
that Daphnis' experience of Eros destroyed him. And there is indeed a close parallel in the *Pastoral Idylls* to this evocation of the
destructive effects of passion. In *Idyll XI* we learned that once the
legendary one-eyed Cyclops Polyphemus, a herdsman like Daphnis,
and like Daphnis a pastoral poet, was in love with Galatea (*XI* l.8).
The story, told in the simplest manner possible by Theocritus, starts
out the same way as the account of Daphnis in *Idyll VII*:
"Polyphemus . . . loved Galatea." Polyphemus was no ordinary
lover: his love led him to the very edge of insanity (*orthais maniais*
11). Thus his passion for Galatea was potentially a very destructive
one.

The important difference between this story and the story of Daphnis lies in the ending: Daphnis wastes away, whereas Polyphemus "found the remedy" for the disease which threatened him. Theocritus is very explicit as to the nature of that remedy: Polyphemus composed a song (which is given in *XI* ll. 19 - 79), and this song cured him, protected him from the destructive effects of his passion for Galatea. Polyphemus, unlike Daphnis, was not destroyed by his experience of Eros, but rather was able to sublimate that Eros into song.

It is important to note that although Polyphemus addresses Galatea as an ordinary "girl" (*kora XI* l. 25), there is really nothing ordinary about her. Galatea is a sportive nymph who spies on Polyphemus from the waves of her watery home (cf. *VI* ll. 27 - 28), she is an elusive will-o'-the-wisp who appears in his dreams; finally, she is a spirit who teases Polyphemus, and inspires him with a passion that is impossible to gratify in any ordinary sexual manner. Like the Galatea of Raphael's luminous painting, Theocritus' Galatea is the fresh and semidivine embodiment of all that is beautiful ·and alluring. The courtship of Polyphemus and Galatea symbolizes the eternal pursuit of beauty by the poet; this lighthearted confrontation is destined to go on without ever reaching the goal which human lovers set for themselves. Galatea is Polyphemus' teasing, playful Muse. His response to her beauty is a song, not an embrace.

Daphnis, however, did not find salvation in poetry. It is clear from both the accounts—*Idylls I* and *VII*—that Daphnis wasted away in silence, a silence that contrasted with the loud lamentations of Nature at his approaching death. The absence of the Nymphs is perhaps the most ominous indication that things are going very badly with Daphnis. The Nymphs are the inspirers of poetry; in *Idyll VII* ll. 91 - 93 Simichidas says that "the Nymphs taught me many other excellent songs while I tended my herds on the hill." In Theocritus they seem to serve the same function as the Muses—the Muses who are the only "cure for love" in *Idyll XI*.[9] When the Nymphs abandoned Daphnis to his fate, that was the end of Daphnis as a poet. Since Daphnis was also in love (with the nymph Xenea), he was left defenseless against the destructive effects of passion, and perished. Only the Nymphs and song could have saved him—the two elements so conspicuously lacking in the description of his final hour in *Idyll I* and so conspicuously present in *Idyll XI*.

From this Theocritean perspective it is possible to understand the anguish of Daphnis as humorously described by Priapus. The "girl" who is frantically searching for him is a threatening figure; her love for him has become a source of torment, as Hermes guesses in line 78. If she is looking so carefully for him, we can assume that soon she will find him on the banks of the Anapus. Daphnis' death, under the circumstances, looks like a suicide designed to allow him an escape from love in death: "Even in Hades I will be the bitter enemy of Eros," he says to Aphrodite (103). Daphnis is also tormented by the fact that he cannot join in the dance of the laughing maidens (90 - 91), and here it is possible to agree with Williams that these maidens are the Nymphs.[10] The dance of the maidens represents for Daphnis that playful creative spirit which has abandoned him; he has lost his contact with the springs of poetic inspiration, and this is his greatest misfortune. Priapus and Aphrodite, the representatives of unsublimated Eros, cannot help him in the absence of the Nymphs, who alone can sponsor creative sublimation. In the Theocritean pastoral world, only the powers of creative sublimation could have saved him, as is demonstrated most clearly in the case of Polyphemus in *Idyll XI*.

The reason for the moribund Daphnis' rage against Aphrodite is now clear: the fatal passion that she inspired in the girl for him (the Greeks saw Aphrodite as the cause of all such passionate excesses) destroyed him as a bucolic poet. All that is left for Daphnis (since song is denied him) is to call on Pan to receive the Syrinx from his dying hands (123 - 30); this is his final act, and marks the end of his career as a poet. There is something tragically heroic in Daphnis' refusal to live on after his genius has been destroyed, which explains why the story of Daphnis is so moving for the herdsmen-poets of *Idyll I*. But there is also a morbid side to the story. A feeling of horror grows in us as Daphnis, putting aside the dignified silence with which he greeted the concern of his herdsmen friends and the witticisms of Priapus, raises his voice in feeble retaliation against the jibes of the goddess Aphrodite (95 - 113). His snide remarks, charged with exacerbated feelings of personal resentment, reveal him as a dying man whose poetic genius has decayed into a morbid preoccupation with—and neurotic hostility to—the claims of Eros. If the figure of Gustav von Aschenbach comes to mind, it is because in *Death in Venice* Thomas Mann has described the horror as well as the glory of an artist's confrontation with the power of Eros which overwhelms him and causes his death. Daphnis and Aschenbach have much in common.

Theocritus has used the myth of Daphnis in a very original and personal way; that is, he has put emphasis on those elements of the myth which suit his purpose, and has left other elements obscure. The traditional story of Daphnis, whatever it may have been exactly, is transformed by Theocritus into a Theocritean myth, a myth which is the tragic counterpart of the Theocritean myth of Polyphemus. What Theocritus strove to express in the parallel myths of Daphnis and Polyphemus, was his sense that the step beyond ordinary existence that the poet takes when he dares to follow the creative impulse within him, is fraught with danger. The sublimation of Eros, which allows the poet to produce that which Diotima in the *Symposium* called "spiritual children" (his poems),[11] for all that it creates a heightening of consciousness and a sharpening of the creative powers, involves a potentially disastrous withdrawal from instinctual involvement with life. Unless harmony is established between the instincts and the powers of creative sublimation, the poet may be destroyed, like Daphnis, in the clash of opposing forces: Life against Art, Eros against the Nymphs.

But *Idyll I* does not end on a morbid or a tragic note. As soon as Thyrsis has finished the Daphnis song, he asks for the cup which the goatherd promised him as a reward for his singing. Thyrsis will use this cup (a symbol of Theocritus' pastoral art, as we have seen) to pour a libation of milk to the Muses (143 - 45). The cheerful symbolism of this cup dedicated to the worship of the Muses stands in sharp contrast to the tragic tale of Daphnis. In the last lines of *Idyll I* (146 - 52), the goatherd's warm words of appreciation for the song which he was privileged to hear, the sweet smell of the freshly carved wooden cup, and the final image (152) of the virile billy goat, combine to create a brief evocation of a pastoral world where art and life are in perfect harmony.

II   Idyll III *("The Serenade")*

In this pastoral idyll an unnamed goatherd, aping the city custom of the nocturnal serenade, goes to the cave of Amaryllis and sings. The song (6 - 51) is framed by the goatherd's own introductory and concluding remarks (1 - 5, 52 - 54), and is twice interrupted (24, 37 - 39) by his asides.

Theocritus' most obvious intention in this idyll, all commentators agree, was to write a pastoral parody of the *kōmos* and the song which usually accompanied it, the *paraklausithyron*. The term *kōmos* refers to a custom followed especially by city-bred young men before they married; they would wind up an evening spent drinking and partying by sallying forth in a small group to serenade the latest flame of one of their number. If the serenade was successful, the beloved's door would open, and the lover would find the reward of his sleepless vigil and serenading; this serenade was part of the courtship game in which lighthearted and passionate lovers alike were expected to engage, if they expected to win the affection of a young boy or an unmarried woman of easy virtue. Theocritus describes such a nocturnal expedition in *Idyll II* ll. 118 - 28, although in that example the young lady was already so willing that no *kōmos* was actually needed to inspire her with pity for her lover's plight. In *Idyll VII*, another *kōmos* is described (*VII* ll. 122 - 27), but the boy is unyielding, and Theocritus-Simichidas is clearly bored by the prospect of spending another night seconding his friend Aratus' sexual adventures.

The *kōmos* was an interesting topic for epigrams, and a small number of such short literary treatments of the theme have been preserved. The actual serenade or *paraklausithyron* (literally, "a song sung before a locked door") was frequently the element most imitated, as in the following epigram by Theocritus' contemporary at the Museum in Alexandria, Callimachus:

> I hope you sleep as badly as you make me sleep,
> Conopion, on the cold stones of your front porch.
> I hope you sleep, you dreadful tease, the way
> you make your lover sleep—without a dream of pity.
> Your neighbors pity me, but you can't even dream of it.
> (Callimachus, *Epigram LXIV* ll. 1 - 5)

At the end of *Idyll III*, the goatherd-lover threatens to lie down on the ground and never get up—a traditional ending for a *kōmos*. But he fails to realize that standing or lying in front of the open entrance of Amaryllis' cave simply makes him look ridiculous: the door is open, or rather, there is no door except a screen of vegetation through which a bee could easily buzz (12 - 14). The goatherd merits none of the pity which an urban lover and *kōmastēs* could arouse, who is kept out in the cold all night by the bolted door, since, as far as we can tell, the goatherd's serenade takes place in broad daylight. All in all, the goatherd cuts a poor and ridiculous figure. It is hardly surprising that Amaryllis fails to respond to his pathetic serenade.[12]

The second part of the goatherd's inept *paraklausithyron* contains a series of references to mythology (40 - 51). Presumably such impressively learned references were intended by the goatherd to impress Amaryllis with his sophistication as well as to provide her with reasons for giving in to his desires, since Greek mythology contained so many examples of amorous daring among the gods and heroes.

The following epigram by Asclepiades (or Sicelidas) of Samos, a contemporary poet whose verse Theocritus praises highly in *Idyll VII* ll. 39 - 40, is a good example of how such a learned allusion could be used effectively:

> Send down snow upon me—hail—darkness—lightning—thunder!
> Let the black clouds gather and blanket the earth!
> Kill me! and I'll stop. But if you let me live,
> I'll get through worse than this to sing my serenade.
> The god who is my master is also yours, O Zeus:
> because of him you turned yourself to gold to enter
>   brazen chambers.
> (*Palatine Anthology*, v.64)

In this epigram the passionate *kōmastēs* takes Zeus as his model. Zeus once found a way to make love to Danae, whose father had imprisoned her behind the brazen doors of a dungeon (not even axes or torches would have helped in this case), by taking the form of a golden shower of rain. Asclepiades' use of the myth is especially elegant and witty. The lover finds or imagines himself in the middle of a terrible winter storm, which aggravates the usual difficulties and dangers (darkness, cold, fatigue, and muggers) which traditionally beset a lover on his nocturnal trek through the city streets to his beloved's door. Zeus was commonly held responsible for such meteorological phenomena, and the lover has to remind Zeus that even the king of the gods was subject to the commands of Eros the god of Love; given the storm which threatens the lover, the allusion to Zeus' metamorphosis into a gold shower is doubly witty and appropriate to the situation.

The goatherd's use of mythology in *Idyll III*, by comparison, is comically inept. He has brought love apples to Amaryllis (10 - 11), and this apparently inspires his reference to Atalanta in lines 40 - 42: Hippomenes won the heart of this reluctant female athlete with the magic assistance of golden apples provided by Aphrodite. However, the poor goatherd's apples are hardly golden, and Amaryllis herself had to tell him where to pick them (10 - 11). No doubt Bias won the hand of Peiro (the future mother of Alphesiboea) with a herd of cattle which his brother Melampus rounded up (Homer tells the story in *Odyssey XI* ll. 281 - 98), but the nanny goat and two kids which the goatherd offers Amaryllis (34 - 36) hardly stand comparison with a herd (43 - 45)! Once again the goatherd puts his foot in his mouth with comically inappropriate allusions to myth and legend.

The last three allusions in the goatherd's series are as pompous as the allusion to Zeus in Asclepiades' epigram, but they lack the wit which would make the hyperbole entertaining. In addition, the three allusions to divine amorous adventures have extremely disquieting undertones. Adonis (46 - 48) won the love of the goddess Aphrodite, but soon after came to a violent end, gored to death by a wild boar. Endymion (49 - 50) was the favorite of the moon goddess Selene—but why should the goatherd "envy" the eternal sleep to which Selene's love condemned him? The last allusion is no doubt the most preposterous. Iasion (50 - 51) no doubt played a role in the mysteries of Demeter; but when the goatherd boasts that the story is one that the uninitiated will never know (51), the Greek reader, initiated or not, would have been just as likely to remember the story of Iasion which Homer told in the fifth book of the *Odyssey* (V ll. 125 - 28):

> Then Demeter of the tasseled tresses yielded
> to Iasion, mingling and making love
> in a furrow three times plowed; but Zeus found out
> and killed him with a white-hot thunderbolt.
>   (translated by Robert Fitzgerald)

The goatherd hardly intends to share such a fate, but the art of learned allusion (an Alexandrian art par excellence) is too complicated for him to master, and he winds up saying more than he wishes to imply.

A reading of *Idyll III* as a sophisticated comic skit or mime about a dumb yokel aping city ways and spouting inappropriate learned allusions to mythology, although it is justified as a primary reading, does not, to my mind, exhaust the possibilities of interpretation. One problem remains unsolved by this generally accepted interpretation of *Idyll III*, and its resolution points to the possibility of a second reading which gives this comic piece of bucolic burlesque a darker thematic coloring.

The problem lies in the ultimate identity of Amaryllis. Commentators have too hastily assumed that Amaryllis is some country girl to whom the goatherd is paying court. But if it is ridiculous for a goatherd to sing a *paraklausithyron* in front of an entrance to a cave, it is equally strange that Amaryllis should be living there in the first place. Young girls of marriageable age did not live by themselves in caves, although conceivably a shepherd boy might seek shelter in one from time to time. In addition, Amaryllis' cave shows no signs of human habitation: its entrance is covered over with vegetation (cf. "the ivy and the ferns which hide you from my sight" 14). Such a cave would hardly be a fit dwelling place for the lovely Amaryllis—unless, of course, she happened to be a nymph. Nymphs were often worshipped in caves; two caves described in the *Odyssey* were inhabited by nymphs (Calypso's cave in *Odyssey* V ll. 57 - 63, and the cave of the nymphs in *Odyssey* XIII ll. 103 - 12, whose bees and hidden divinities are reminiscent of *Idyll III* ll. 12 - 14).[13] The goatherd addresses Amaryllis on two occasions as *Nympha* (9, 19); Gow translates "maiden" in both cases, and Dover glosses the term as follows: "Amaryllis is not a supernatural 'nymph' but a human girl, whom the goatherd addresses as 'bride.' "[14] However, *nympha* implies semidivine status just as readily as marriageability (cf. Stanford's note on *Odyssey* VI l. 123); and the first meaning, for the reasons stated above, makes better sense in the context of *Idyll III*.

If Amaryllis is in fact a nymph, the tragic implications of the goatherd's allusions to the fate of lovers of immortal goddesses (Adonis, Endymion and Iasion), although unintended by the goatherd himself, are perhaps not so ridiculous after all. It is appropriate to recall at this juncture that Daphnis also alluded to the story of Adonis (*I* ll. 105 - 10), probably with a full sense of its tragic analogy with his own bitter fate. If the goatherd, like Daphnis, Endymion, Iasion, and Adonis, is in love with a female divinity, then he is by symbolic implication venturing into that dangerous realm beyond the pale of ordinary human experience which the poet enters when he seeks the inspiration of the Nymphs and Muses. For all his silly posturing and inept singing, the goatherd-poet of *Idyll III* is an ironic protagonist who plays a serious role, and even a potentially tragic one, for in the realm of the conflict of Art and Life, insanity and death await the poet just as readily as the vision of beauty. Amaryllis symbolizes, as a nymph never seen but always sought, that vision of beauty; she is the goatherd-poet's semi-divine source of inspiration. The threat of suicide, however comically it is introduced in lines 9 and 25 - 27, can be taken as a genuinely somber motif connected with the Theocritean vision of the artist's life which encompasses "the sufferings of Daphnis" as much as the poet's creative joy.

Let us examine the last lines of *Idyll III*, and consider how they might be interpreted from the two perspectives we have taken into account.

> Now I've got a headache, but you don't care! I'll
>   sing no more—
> I'll just lie down where I've fallen, and the wolves
>   will come and eat me.
> I hope *that* will be just like honey going down your throat!

If *Idyll III* is only a clever burlesque of a kōmos and *paraklausithyron*, then these lines parody the urban lover's final gesture of lying down to sleep on the threshold of his beloved's dwelling *(thyraulia)* as a sign of faithfulness and determination. A headache is about all the suffering the silly goatherd can tolerate, and we are sure that he would run at the sight of a wolf! But viewing the final lines from the second perspective which I have proposed, the section appears as a comic and ironic presentation of a tragic bucolic theme, according to which the herdsman-poet courts death when he seeks to bridge the gap between the human and the divine, and woos a beautiful but perhaps deadly nymph.

III   Idyll IV *("Battus and Corydon")*

Idyll IV takes the form of a rambling conversation between two herdsmen, Battus and Corydon. The scene is set near Kroton, a Greek city in southern Italy. Corydon is taking care of the cattle which Aegon has left behind in his search for glory at the Olympian Games. Battus criticizes the poor condition of the herd. The two talk on, discussing Aegon's syrinx, which Corydon is now playing; the dead Amaryllis, whose memory fills Battus with nostalgia; the straying cattle; and the sexual life of Aegon's father. That is all—a country conversation. Is it possible that Theocritus could have been content with so little?

The relative formlessness and apparent simplicity of *Idyll IV* are as much an artistic ploy as the allusiveness of *Idyll I* or the broad parodic humor of *Idyll III*. The poem can be enjoyed on several levels. The interpretation of the idyll depends on what type of analysis is attempted. The conversation can be appreciated for its dramatic movement, economy, and variety; it can be equally well enjoyed for the contrasting psychological and emotional states to which the characters give expression. A thematic analysis of the poem can be the stimulus for a second look at its apparently casual structure. In the final analysis, *Idyll IV* is not as transparently simple as it first appears.

The dramatic movement and pacing of *Idyll IV* can be described in a few words. The first section (1 - 14) consists of rapid single-line repartee (stichomythia), question and answer, thrust and parry. The second section (15 - 28) is marked by somewhat longer verbal exchanges of two or three lines each. The third section (29 - 43) contains what is for this idyll a long speech (29 - 37) and two three-line exchanges (38 - 43); the long speech occupies the central position in the poem. The fourth section (44 - 57) creates a little flurry of dramatic action: the cattle are straying, and Battus gets a thorn in his foot. The fifth section (58 - 63) returns to the question and answer pattern of the opening, in three exchanges of three lines each. It should be clear from this outline that *Idyll IV* consists of four movements of equal length (14 - 15 lines) with a shorter finale; that it begins and ends quickly; and that the longest speech occupies the center of gravity of the idyll. There is thus a structured variety in *Idyll IV* and an element of aesthetic control over the material which manifests itself in the artful dramatic pacing and length of the exchanges. This artfulness prevents the poem from lapsing into the formlessness of an actual conversation. Dramatic action interrupts the flow of conversation (section four), which is reestablished in the concluding verses, but only briefly.

Part of the charm of *Idyll IV* derives from the contrasting emotional makeup of the two protagonists. Corydon is consistently cheerful, optimistic, present-oriented, and practical. Battus, on the other hand, starts out with a good deal of latent hostility toward Corydon; he is also full of nostalgic regret for Aegon who has left for Olympia, and for Amaryllis who is dead; his gloomy nostalgia verges on depression. But at the end of the idyll, Corydon has won him over to a more cheerful view of life.

Battus is initially afraid of the challenges of life beyond the *locus amoenus*. For him, Aegon's decision to compete in the Olympian Games is a tragic one: "O ill-fated Aegon, your cattle are also on the road to Hades, since even you have become obsessed with stupid dreams of glory" (26 - 27). In the first two sections of the poem, Battus sees only the dark side of the situation: Aegon's cattle are wasting away from grief over their master's absence, and Corydon is too incompetent to take Aegon's place in caring for them properly. But Corydon does not get angry at this unjustified criticism; rather, he takes it on himself to slowly bring Battus out of the mood which has taken possession of him, and to cure him of his melancholy. It is true, he admits, that Aegon's cattle are refusing to eat (14) because they feel despondent over Aegon's departure (12), but Corydon is doing his best to care for them (17 - 19, 23 - 25). But it is when Battus complains that Aegon's syrinx is getting mildewed from disuse and neglect (28) that Corydon has a real chance to counter Battus' mood of eternal pessimism, and launches into a long, enthusiastic tirade:

> "Not so, by the Nymphs, not so! when Aegon left for Olympia,
> he gave those pipes to *me!* I am a bit of a singer myself,—
> I can do Glauke's songs well and Pyrrus' songs well, too."
>   (ll. 29 - 31)

Since the connection between singing and piping is likely to be puzzling to the modern reader, I should explain that Corydon would play a few notes on the syrinx, sing a few lines, pipe again, sing again—much like Papageno in Mozart's *Magic Flute*. But even Greek readers must have been surprised that Corydon, a herdsman from South Italy, should be so well acquainted with the verses of Glauke, an Alexandrian poetess who apparently flourished during the reign of Ptolemy Philadelphus.

What has happened here is that the thematic emphasis of the poem has shifted from regret for the athlete Aegon (who also turns out to be a bucolic musician) to a celebration of poetry. The longest speech in *Idyll IV* is dedicated to this new theme, which through the central position of the speech is presented as the central theme of the idyll. This enthusiastic evocation of the joys of poetic creativity is Corydon's response to the dismal jeremiads of Battus, just as the appeal to the Nymphs (29) is his immediate rejoinder to the images of death ("Hades" 27) and decay (the mildewed syrinx, 28) evoked by his gloomy companion.

A second theme is introduced at the same time. Corydon, who seems to be on the verge of improvising a song in honor of Aegon

(33 - 37), is ready to celebrate the legendary courtship of Aegon and Amaryllis, a story which took place *in illo tempȯre*, once upon a time, when Aegon, a Greek Paul Bunyan, could devour eighty loaves of bread at a sitting, and drag a bull from the field by the hoof and give it to Amaryllis as a present.

Battus' reaction to this story (38 - 40) is predictably and perversely morbid: Amaryllis is dead, and we'll never forget her—mine is a cruel, cruel fate and an unhappy destiny (the lines in Greek are ridiculously bathetic). Poetic visions of a happier world only remind him of how dismal things are today. Corydon is forced to lecture him about his neurotic tendency to despair and depression, although the lecture consists, humorously enough, of a Hesiodic string of pious platitudes (41 - 43). But they are enough to get Battus out of the dumps, and when Battus says, "Now I am feeling more cheerful" (*tharseō* 44), it is a sign that his gloom has lifted, thanks to Corydon's patient efforts to cheer him up.

The scene where Battus suddenly steps on a thorn (50 - 57) is a symbolic reenactment of the earlier conversation. Battus has fallen on the thorns of life, and Corydon, who pulls out the thorn, reminds him that it is not wise to walk barefoot on the hill, where thorns and brambles grow in profusion. By now Battus has learned to take things cheerfully in stride, and his final exchange with Corydon has none of the latent hostility of the first one. Battus questions Corydon about Aegon's father (cf. 4), and is delighted to hear that the old man still loves the ladies (58 - 63), and that he is "grinding away" ("mullei" 58) at his girlfriend of long standing.

A thematic analysis of *Idyll IV* raises several interesting issues. The actual motifs are usually introduced by careful transitions, but they seem at first glance to bear little relation to each other. The first section is dominated by the motif of the boxer Aegon who has abandoned the pastoral world for the opportunity of winning glory at the Olympian games (1 - 11). The transition to the second motif is found in the last three lines of the stychomythia, starting with Corydon's remark that Aegon's cattle are filled with longing (*potheunti* 12) for their absent master. Their refusal to eat, the motif of the next section (15 - 28), is thus an animal manifestation of what, in humans, would be diagnosed as an obvious symptom of love-sickness; in all events, Corydon and Battus, who as herdsmen ought to know, consider this to be a reasonable diagnosis. Battus' remark about Aegon's supposedly mildewed syrinx (which is associated in his mind with starving cattle) provides the transition to the next motif, the celebration of poetry and music of lines 29 - 37. The mention of the name of Amaryllis triggers the appearance of the next motif: the dead Amaryllis. Dramatic action interrupts thematic accumulation during lines 45 - 57, although the thorns constitute a pretty kind of dramatic symbol by themselves. The poem ends with the motif of the sexually vigorous old man (58 - 63).

Thematically, it must be admitted, *Idyll IV* is a puzzle. Motifs are introduced and then replaced almost haphazardly. The poem is kaleidoscopic in its rapid switch from one motif to another. However, several major themes emerge, which preside over the organization of the motifs and constitute their *raison d'être*.

One theme is the theme of "time lost"—*le temps perdu*. Battus confronts a world where all that he considers valuable has been swept away by time: Aegon has left the country, Amaryllis is dead, and life hardly seems worth living anymore. The cattle's "longing" for Aegon finds its human parallel in Battus' regret for the dead Amaryllis; even the otherwise rather bathetic comparison he uses (Amaryllis was as dear to him as his goats, 36) reinforces the parallel.

Corydon is the chief spokesman for the second theme. Corydon, as it turns out rather unexpectedly, is very much the Theocritean herdsman-poet. His long and enthusiastic praise of himself as poet in the central section of *Idyll IV* includes the sketch of a longer song which would have dealt with the courtship of the hero Aegon and the lovely Amaryllis. The theme of the recapturing of the past through art (*"le temps retrouvé"*—although one must be careful not to push the Proustian analogy too far) fails to make much of an obvious impression on Battus; nevertheless it is connected thematically with his sudden good spirits at the end of the poem. The image of the sexually vigorous old man, whose age does not rule out youthful ardor, whose "past," that is, does not rule out the joys of the present, is another sign of that interpenetration of past and present which art can celebrate when it recaptures the past. The phrase which Battus is inspired to introduce, regretfully in the context—"O lovely Amaryllis"—is in fact the opening of the goatherd's song in *Idyll III* (*"ō chariess' Amarulli" III* l.6 and *IV* l.38), and is thus as unwittingly artful as it is nostalgic. Nevertheless, it is Corydon who is the true bucolic poet in *Idyll IV*. His cheerfulness, friendliness, enthusiasm, and love of poetry (imagine a goatherd who knows about Glauke! Theocritus seems to imply in line 31) link him with such figures as the goatherd and

Thyrsis in *Idyll I*. Battus, on the other hand, with his morbid regret for Aegon and Amaryllis, reminds us of the darker and more dangerous side of life in the *locus amoenus*, where depression, love-sickness, decay of genius, and death stalk the unwary herdsman. Thanks to Corydon, Battus escapes all but a touch of these pastoral diseases of the soul.

The pastoral art of Theocritus is frequently an art of ironic understatement, and never more so than in *Idyll IV*. Its sentimentality, humor, bathos, as well as the absence of a strongly articulated structure, are signs of a subtle and light orchestration of some of the major themes of Theocritus' evocation of the artist's life in the *locus amoenus*.

IV   Idyll V (*"Comatas and Lacon"*)

In *Idyll V*, Comatas the goatherd and the young shepherd Lacon meet by chance, and engage in a singing match, with Morson the woodcutter as their judge. Comatas wins. This long idyll consists of a conversational frame (1 - 79, 138 - 50), and of the amoebaean verses (couplets sung alternatively) of the singing match (80 - 137), during which Lacon tries to "cap" the couplets which Comatas improvises.

Comatas and Lacon are former lovers, and the singing match can be viewed as a sublimated reenactment of their earlier sexual encounters (41 - 42,   116 - 17). This line of interpretation, first suggested by Lawall ("Song has not banished the herdsmen's passions but has channeled them toward a temporary resolution"),[15] is helpful in understanding the antagonistic and charged atmosphere of *Idyll V*, where the bitter rivalry of the two herdsmen-poets has a sexual as well as an artistic dimension. But there is no need to dwell exclusively on the element of erotic strife, since behind the particular manifestation of the theme of homosexual aggression lies the more general theme of the creative sublimation of the sexual instincts.

One of the major themes, if not *the* major theme, of the *Pastoral Idylls*, is the creative sublimation of the sexual instincts, by means of which the pastoral protagonist becomes somewhat less of a lover as he becomes more of a poet. The theme must be properly understood. To merely state that "love inspires song" is to sentimentalize and trivialize what is a quite sophisticated theme. Song is as much a way of avoiding love as of expressing love in the *Pastoral*

Idylls. Yet there is nothing neurotic or repressive about this avoidance: song results from consciously and freely choosing to transfer energy from the purely sexual level to the creative level. This sublimation of sexual energy transforms sexual Eros into creative Eros. Daphnis in *Idyll I* was a tragic figure, precisely because Eros "dragged him down to Hades" (cf. *I* l. 130)—the very opposite of what we have described as creative sublimation of Eros.

The figure of Comatas in *Idyll V* stands in extreme contrast to the tragic figure of Daphnis. "The Muses love me far more than the singer Daphnis," sings Comatas in his first amoebaean couplet (80 - 81), and these words are the key to his place in Theocritus' pastoral mythology. A detailed analysis of *Idyll V* from the general perspective of the theme of creative sublimation, should make clear why Theocritus chose this foul-smelling (51 - 52), sexually aggressive and extremely vain goatherd for the role of archetypal pastoral poet.

Idyll V opens with a bitter squabble between the two main protagonists (1 - 20). Comatas accuses Lacon of filching his goatskin cloak, and Lacon complains in turn that Comatas stole his syrinx. The word "syrinx" occurs three times in lines 4 - 6; as in *Idyll IV* (cf. Aegon's syrinx, *IV* l. 28 ff.), the motif is used to introduce the theme of poetry into the debate. The stolen goatskin turns out to be another such symbolic motif, since Crocylus gave it to Comatas after he had sacrificed the goat to the Nymphs, the inspirers of song in Theocritus' pastoral world. Comatas swears by the Nymphs (17, 70); and when Lacon wishes to persuade him to come over and sit with him next to the wild olive tree (cf. 32), he offers to set a bowl of milk and a bowl of oil as an offering for Comatas' favorite deities (53 - 54). Lacon himself swears by Pan (14) and, more sinisterly, by "the sufferings of Daphnis"—as in the opening of *Idyll I*, the better poet of the two swears by the Nymphs, not by Pan the herdsmen's god.

The acrimonious conversation shifts to a new topic in line 21, when Lacon proposes a singing match. Comatas' reaction is typically belligerent and vain: "a pig once tried to compete with Athena" (23), and Lacon is a "a wasp who buzzes against a cicada" (cicadas were much appreciated for their sounds, cf. the cricket of *Idyll I* l. 52). At the end of the contest (136 - 37) Comatas will add the comparisons of jays competing with nightingales, and hoopoes with swans (swans sang beautifully and for the first time at their dying hour, the Greeks believed). As in the opening of *Idyll I*, the contestants argue over where they should sit down and sing (31 - 61), but here the conflict is never resolved; each stays where he is, since each has a good reason for wishing to avoid the shady spot which his opponent cleverly proposes. As we learn in lines 118 - 19 near the end of the contest, the wild olive tree under which Lacon is sitting has humiliating associations for Comatas: it was to that tree that his boss Eumaras once tied him and gave him a memorable whipping. And Lacon himself is none too eager to go over to the oaks to whose shade Comatas invites him, since one of those oaks, we learn in lines 116 - 17, witnessed a violent love scene between him and Comatas which he pretends not to remember.

Why are the two herdsmen acting in such a belligerent manner? The issue revolves around the notion of *paideia*, at least initially. It was customary in ancient Greece for an older man who had developed a particular liking for a boy to take him under his protection, and see to his proper education (*paideia*). Thus in Theocritus' *Idyll XIII* the hero Herakles "was in love with a boy, the lovely Hylas . . . and like a father teaching his own son, taught his beloved all those things which had helped him to become a famous hero" (*XIII* ll. 6 - 9).[16] Comatas claims to have seen to Lacon's education in this Greek sense of the term, and charges the independent-minded Lacon with ingratitude: "it is most painful for me to see how little respect you have for me [lit. "how you look me straight in the eye"], when it was I who taught you everything when you were just a boy" (35 - 37). But Lacon is not about to yield to Comatas' sentimental attempt to reassert his former authority over him:

> Lacon: And when was it that I ever learned anything
> worthwhile from you—you envious beast!
> Comatas: When I buggered you, and you cried out in pain,
> and these very same nanny-goats began to bleat, and
> the he-goat mounted them.
> (ll. 39 - 42)

Such, apparently, was the value of Comatas' *paideia* for Lacon, as far as both of them are now concerned! Theocritus does not usually use such direct language, but here the obscene is necessary in order to indicate the raw sexual emotions which are reawakened in the present confrontation of the two herdsmen.

Given the context, it would seem obvious that Lacon proposed the singing match partly in order to get back at Comatas for his earlier sexual domination over him; he is seeking to humiliate his former lover and mentor by winning the match. However, Theocritus allows Comatas to carry off the prize instead, as if to indicate with the utmost clarity that the singing match is a sublimated version of the earlier sexual contest, in which the older goatherd played the dominant and aggressive role. Thus Comatas, when challenged by Lacon to defend his reputation as a singer, reacts as vigorously and as aggressively as a poet as he once did as a lover.

It is reasonable to assume that the singing contest in *Idyll V* reflects to some degree actual customs of Greek herdsmen, which in modern Sicily seem to have survived unchanged. Gavin Maxwell, in a book on Sicilian life written in the 1950s *(The Ten Pains of Death)*, transcribed the account which a young Sicilian herdsman, Nenè, gave of his life in the fields. In the following quotation, the fifteen-year-old cowherd describes the *botta e risposta* kind of singing which was practiced among herdsmen of his age; there is no formal contest of the sort we find in *Idyll V*, but the reader will notice the same art of invective and capping couplets, as well as the stylized sexual boasting and abuse of one's cosinger which Maxwell (like Gow) chose not to translate into English. As in *Idyll V* (although not for the same reasons), the two opponents sing to each other over a distance.

Then there's songs you sing in alternate verses with someone you can hear but most times can't see. These are called *botta e risposta*. We herds don't often meet each other in the mountains—each of us takes his animals to different places because there's not enough grass to go round, but we can play games together even if we're far apart. You hear the voice of another herd singing far away and you wait for the right moment and answer him. If he hears you start up alternate verses like this:

> I sing: Who are you that's singing up there?
>   You sound like a yapping puppy.
> And he answers:
>   And who are you wailing away down there?
>   You sound as if you had toothache in every tooth.
> I: When you were born behind my door
>   I thought you were a still-born bitch-pup.
> He: When you were born in the middle of my street
>   There was an awful stink of dung.

The author ceases to translate Nenè's couplets, noting that "they end in a perfect orgy of sexual abuse and sexual boasting."[17]

However, the element of actual hostility is carefully "sublimated" in this case as well: "We don't take offense at what we sing to each other—if we did we wouldn't sing them, or else we'd go and beat each other up."[18]

Lacon and Nenè have another experience in common. "Don Paolo's fond of me. . . . One day when I was ten and I was at the farm where I used to wash dishes, Don Paolo was in the cowshed and he called me, and—a thing he'd never made me do—he made me milk the cows. I was pleased, because at that time the only person there who was allowed to milk the cows was Zu Aspanu. And then Don Paolo . . . [follows a description of his seduction by Don Paolo]. Then I began to understand, because one does understand these things by oneself—and Don Paolo told me some things too. If Don Paolo hadn't told me I'd have known just the same, because we boys talk among ourselves the whole time."[19] The employer Don Paolo played roughly the role which was delegated to Comatas in *Idyll V*, in which *paideia* is viewed mainly as sexual initiation.

The actual singing match between Comatas and Lacon (80 - 137) raises several questions of interpretation. First of all, what justifies Comatas' victory? The question has already been answered, in my opinion, by the thematic necessity of linking Comatas' past sexual domination over Lacon to his victory over his younger opponent in the poetic sphere of activity as well. Still, the question remains: is there anything in the singing match itself which justifies Morson's decision to award the prize to Comatas?

John Van Sickle sees Comatas' truthfulness as one reason why the prize should go to him.[20] In *Idyll VII* l. 44 Lycidas praises Simichidas for the truthfulness *(alatheia)* of his nature; in *Idyll V*, Comatas does not disguise the fact from Morson that both he and Lacon do not own the animals they are caring for; and when Lacon becomes irritated and embarrassed over this revelation of his status as a mere hired hand, Comatas replies (76): "My dear fellow, I tell the whole truth." The question then arises as to whether Comatas was telling the truth when he denied having stolen Lacon's pipe (5 ff). The word "syrinx" appears again in line 135, in the last couplet which Morson allows Lacon to sing: "But I am head over heels in love with Eumedes, since when I gave him/ the syrinx, he went straight ahead and kissed me." It may be poetic justice, I think, that Morson stops Lacon after this couplet; although Morson was not there to witness the first altercation between the herdsmen-poets, the reader remembers that syrinx, and now has no further cause to suspect Comatas of the theft, since it appears that Lacon had simply given the instrument to one of his boy loves of the moment.

Gilbert Lawall has pointed out how, in the couplets of the singing match, Comatas is preoccupied uniquely with girls (a switch from his former preferences), whereas Lacon is now doing to boys (cf. 86 - 87) what Comatas once did to him.[21] Comatas' preference for girls would have been no sign, in the Greek world, of greater sensitivity or status as a lover.

But there is another thing worth noticing in the first couplets he sings in praise of the "girl" (*pais*—she must be young) Clearista. She is a friendly girl, who makes the first advances to him (85), and even totally reverses the usual courting procedure and throws love apples at the older goatherd (88 - 89). There is something, I feel, quite unusual going on here between Comatas and Clearista. No doubt, we hear in another stanza (96 - 97) that Comatas plans to catch a ring dove as a present for his "young woman" (*parthenos*, i.e., a girl of marriageable age), but it turns out later (132 - 33) that the young woman for whom the ring dove was intended, was named Alcippa, not Clearista. It appears that Comatas had another gift in mind for the "girl" (*paidi* again in 105), a gift of a highly unusual sort: a bowl which he calls a "creation of Praxiteles," the outstanding Greek sculptor of the fourth century B.C. Unless Comatas is simply exaggerating (this is one possible interpretation), the gift is totally out of place if Clearista is a simple country girl and Comatas a poor goatherd.

The mystery surrounding Clearista and the strange bowl by Praxiteles is not impenetrable. First of all, Clearista's strange forwardness and apple-throwing is exactly paralleled by the actions of Galatea toward Polyphemus which are the main subjects of both songs in *Idyll VI*. In *Idyll VI* Galatea is clearly a sea-nymph, and her teasing behavior, as I have indicated in my discussion of *Idyll I*, is part of her role of elusive but inspiring Muse. The bowl of *Idyll V* reminds us most of the elaborately sculptured cup in *Idyll I*, which Thyrsis used first in order to make a libation to the Muses. If the reader puts these various symbolic associations together in his mind, remembering that Comatas swears by the Nymphs, and that he will sacrifice the prize lamb to the Nymphs at the end of *Idyll V*, it should be clear that (1) Clearista, like Galatea, is a nymph, that is, a bucolic Muse, and (2) Comatas keeps the pail and the bowl by Praxiteles for her, since he intends to milk one of his goats and pour a libation to her from a sculptured bowl, whose status as a work of art would honor her best as a poet's Muse (cf. the *kratēr* or bowl full of milk for the Nymphs which Lacon is willing to stake, 53 - 54).

Comatas' devotion to Clearista symbolizes his devotion to the Nymphs, that is, his devotion to poetry and song. Lacon has less of such devotion; a symbolic interpretation of his love for Cratidas (the boy he "soils" in the flowers of line 87) is impossible. With the passage of time, Comatas has become more of a poet and less of a lover (although there is always Alcippa, cf. 132). Lacon has grown older and has matured as a lover, but at the present moment he is playing the same role of youthful and passionate lover which Comatas was playing some time before. It is thus perfectly natural, from the Theocritean standpoint, that Comatas, who is certainly more dedicated to his art than Lacon, should carry off the prize.

The final speech of Comatas (141 - 50) is an enthusiastic if rather bizarre self-encomium. Comatas is delighted over his victory, and leaps high into the air in exultation. The rest of his speech makes little sense initially:

> Be cheerful, you horned goats of mine! Tomorrow
> I'll wash every one of you in Sybaris lake.
> And as for *you*, you white, butting billy goat—
> if you mount a nanny goat before I've sacrificed
> the lamb to the Nymphs, I'll castrate you!
>   There he goes again . . . I swear,
> If I don't castrate you, may my name be Melanthius
>   instead of Comatas!
>   (ll. 145 - 50)

As a general rule, anyone sacrificing to the gods should have washed beforehand, especially if sexual intercourse had occurred. However, the rule makes no sense applied to goats—hence, the extravagant humor of the passage.[22] The sexually irrepressible billy goat poses a threat, in Comatas' mind, to the successful outcome of his sacrifice to the Nymphs, and castrating the billy goat would eliminate the problem, such as it is. Comatas even extends the threat of castration to himself in the last line, through his allusion to Melanthius. Melanthius was a goatherd in the *Odyssey* who had sided with the enemies of Odysseus. After the return of Odysseus and his victory over Penelope's suitors, Odysseus and Telemachus dispatched Melanthius with unusual brutality (*Odyssey XXIII* ll. 474 - 77):

> From storeroom to court they brought Melánthios,
> chopped with swords to cut his nose and ears off,
> pulled off his genitals to feed the dogs
> and raging hacked his hands and feet away.
> (translated by Robert Fitzgerald)

In a vivid and unexpectedly concrete manner, this grim motif of castration fits in with the more general theme of creative sublimation which the figure of Comatas, with all his goatish sensuality, has expressed throughout *Idyll V*. The service of the Nymphs requires that Comatas subordinate his amorous pursuits to aesthetic pursuits; in a similar fashion, the sacrifice to the Nymphs requires that the billy goat, the perfect emblem of sexual vigor, restrain himself for a short while, until the sacrifice is over. The last lines of the poem constitute an hilariously grotesque restatement of the major Theocritean theme of the idyll: poetry, like all creative activities, requires a conscious sublimation of the sexual instincts.

V   Idyll VI *("Damoetas and Daphnis")*

Idyll VI depicts a singing match between the cowherds Daphnis and Damoetas. Each herdsman-poet sings a song dealing with the theme of the loves of the Cyclops Polyphemus and the sea nymph Galatea. The idyll consists of a narrative frame (1 - 5, 20, 42 - 46), which defines the clearly amicable and even affectionate spirit of the competition, and the two songs (6 - 19, 21 - 40). The match ends in a draw and an exchange of gifts.

The presentation of the figure of Daphnis in this idyll is perhaps surprising: the tragic figure of *Idyll I* appears in *Idyll VI* as a cheerful teenage cowherd-poet with no problems of his own to worry him. (Daphnis is called *ho boukolos* in line 1, and *ho boutas* in line 44—a sure sign that he is to be identified with the legendary Daphnis the Cowherd of *Idyll I*, cf. *I* ll. 86, 116.) The Daphnis of *Idyll VI* is in fact closer in spirit to the boy on the sculptured cup in *Idyll I;* he has not yet become the lovelorn, death-bound hero of "the sufferings of Daphnis." It is intriguing that Theocritus assigned to this younger, still carefree Daphnis the role of introducing the last of the three major myths of the *Pastoral Idylls* (that is, the Theocritean versions of the myths of Daphnis, Comatas, and Polyphemus), since the comic myth of Polyphemus and Galatea is the structural antithesis of the tragic myth of Daphnis in *Idyll I*.

Idyll VI is addressed to Aratus (2), and Gow has speculated that Theocritus is naming the same Aratus who, in *Idyll VII*, is desperately in love with the boy Philinus (*VII* ll. 98 f.).[23] *Idyll VI* would thus be a fable for Aratus, who, by following the example of the Cyclops, would be more likely to inspire passion in his beloved by feigning indifference than by playing too obviously the role of the passionate and faithful lover.[24] However, it is hard to reconcile the advice which Theocritus supposedly gives Aratus in *Idyll VI* with the cold water which Theocritus throws on passion in *Idyll VII* ("let peace of mind be our chief concern" *VII* l. 126). Furthermore, if Theocritus wished to give advice, he would have stated the moral as in *Idyll XI*, where the Polyphemus story is used to illustrate a moral which is clearly stated (*XI* ll. 1 - 6) and clearly related to the mythological paradigm (*XI* ll. 7 - 8, 80 - 81). Since no such moral is stated in *Idyll VI*, and since the moral, if stated, would hardly be one that Theocritus could be expected to champion, it is better *not* to assume that *Idyll VI* contains a "lesson" which would apply directly to Aratus and his problematic sex life.

Daphnis and Damoetas, the two herdsmen-poets, bring their cattle together near a spring, at the hour of noon (cf. the opening of *Idyll I*). The cattle may well belong to the same herd (*agelan* —"herd"—is in the singular in line 2); if so, this detail reinforces the general sense of the poetic camaraderie and good feeling which characterize their relationship, and which stand in marked contrast to the bickering of Comatas and Lacon in *Idyll V*. Damoetas and Daphnis are of nearly the same age (2 - 3), and both display an equal talent for bucolic improvisation (46). Since the match ends in a draw, both receive prizes: Daphnis gives Damoetas a flute, Damoetas gives him a syrinx, and both begin to pipe away on their new instruments.

Daphnis sings about Polyphemus and Galatea (6 - 19) from the standpoint of a rather puzzled observer of their strange courtship. The gist of his song is a question put to Polyphemus: "Do you not see that Galatea is teasing you, and trying to get your attention and win your affections?" According to the song which Damoetas, impersonating Polyphemus, sings in reply, the one-eyed Cyclops is no blind fool: "Yes, I see her, but I am deliberately teasing her back by feigning indifference to her charms."

Galatea is mentioned in the *Iliad XVIII* l. 45 and in Hesiod's *Theogony* l. 250 as one of the many daughters of the sea god Nereus, the Nereids. Like her sister Thetis, the mother of Achilles,

Galatea was a sea nymph who lived and sported under the waves of the Mediterranean. Etymologically, her name was possibly derived from *gala* or milk; for Eustathius, a Byzantine scholar and commentator of Homer, she was the nymph associated with the milk-white foam of the sea. Nymphs were generally considered to be nature spirits who, like the fairy folk of Celtic mythology, could be helpful as well as harmful to men. Accordingly, they were frequently the objects of local religious cults, and their rustic shrines were a characteristic feature of the Greek landscape. Theocritus, as we have seen, gave the Nymphs in the *Pastoral Idylls* the attributes of rural Muses, who inspired bucolic song and were pleased by the libations of their devoted herdsmen-poets. In *Idylls VI* and *XI*, Galatea is a nymph in the Theocritean sense, that is, a Muse.

The Polyphemus which Homer described in Book IX of the *Odyssey* was a one-eyed giant, one of the lawless and brutal Cyclopes who, according to a later tradition, lived at the Western edge of the Greek world in Sicily. Much is made of Polyphemus' single eye in the middle of his forehead in *Idyll VI* ll. 22 - 24, but it is probably because Theocritus is so preoccupied with visual terms, especially in Damoetas' song where the herdsman-poet is eager to have Polyphemus explain that he really does *see* what Galatea is doing, and also *sees* himself as a handsome fellow when he gazes into the mirrorlike surface of the sea (35 - 38). The loss of sight which the prophet Telemus predicted for him at the hands of Odysseus (*Odyssey IX* ll. 506 - 16) worries him in *Idyll VI* (23 - 24), but, like Daphnis in this idyll, Polyphemus is young, and has not yet experienced the suffering that his mature years will bring to him.

The Cyclops of the *Odyssey* was an unlikely candidate to inspire passion in a beautiful nymph. The figure of an amorous Cyclops was apparently created by the poet Philoxenus at Hiero's court in Syracuse about 400 B.C. (see Chapter 1, section I). His poem or drama on the Cyclops and Galatea was parodied by Aristophanes (*Plutus*, ll. 290 ff.); a short fragment was quoted by Athenaeus (XIII.564E), but otherwise we know only what a few scattered references to the poem can tell us. It appears likely that the Polyphemus of Philoxenus was a ridiculous lovelorn monster, perhaps similar to the portrait which Ovid gives of him in the thirteenth book of the *Metamorphoses*. If so, the originality of Theocritus in *Idyll VI* would be all the more apparent, since Theocritus does not present us with a lovelorn Cyclops, but with a cheerful and jaunty Polyphemus who is being passionately sought after by the nymph Galatea. In *Idyll III* the goatherd courted Amaryllis, and humbly presented her with apples—the ancient equivalent of a box of candy or a Valentine. In *Idyll VI*, the usual role of lover (male, older) and beloved (boy or girl, younger) is reversed: it is Galatea who is bringing apples to Polyphemus (like Clearista in *Idyll V*, Galatea is called a *pais* or "child" in line 13), and what is even more unusual is that she is throwing the apples not at the shepherd, but at the sheep (6 - 7). An odd sort of courtship indeed!

The symbolic dimension of the Theocritean myth of Polyphemus and Galatea accounts for the courtship's strange air of unreality. Galatea is a sea nymph, and Polyphemus, a land-dwelling Cyclops, is both literally and symbolically out of her element. There is no point in interpreting, as Lawall does, this strange courtship as "symbolizing the frustration inherent in actual human relationships."[25] Galatea is, in Theocritean terms, a teasing Muse; in the twentieth century it might help clarify her role and status if we were to borrow a term from Jungian psychology and say that she is an *anima* figure who represents the Eternal Feminine in its inspiring as well as its frustrating and destructive aspects. Her natural element is water, which in Jungian terms symbolizes the Unconscious. Polyphemus is quite right to maintain his land-bound, that is, conscious position; for to follow her into the sea would be to abandon the effort to integrate the unconscious creative energy which Galatea represents, as well as to expose himself to the type of death which Daphnis met in *Idyll I*. Beauty is a semidivine power whose lure the poet must resist as well as celebrate. The "sufferings of Daphnis" await the bucolic poet who yields to the siren song of the *anima:* depression, loss of genius, and death.

It is interesting that it is the young Daphnis of *Idyll VI* who, in his song, fails to understand the defensiveness and seeming indifference with which Polyphemus meets the taunts and blandishments of the lovely nereid. Daphnis is afraid, for example, that the Cyclops' dog (an important motif: cf. 9 - 14, 29 - 30) will "jump at the girl's legs as she comes out of the sea and tear her lovely flesh" (13 - 14)—a remarkably violent image. But Damoetas, who impersonates Polyphemus in his song, and hence sees into the Cyclops' inner motivations, understands immediately why it is that Polyphemus' dog is barking and threatening to bite: "I whistled at the dog to bark at her, because when I was courting her, it used to put its snout on her lap and whine" (29 - 30). The sentimental and

pitiful image of a whining dog reflects exactly the role which
Polyphemus played once as Galatea's suitor; now he is reversing
roles and letting Galatea pursue him while *he* feigns indifference. In
fact, he sics his dog on her, and even threatens to close his door to
any messenger she might send to him (31 - 32). Polyphemus is
determined to force Galatea to join him on the land, to make her
"smoothe out the coverlets of my bed," that is, to become
thoroughly domesticated (33); and this projected domestication of
the Muse is completely consistent with his concern for his own survival and well-being. Damoetas understands all this; Daphnis
presumably never gets the point.

The taunts which Galatea hurls at Polyphemus are disturbingly
reminiscent of Priapus' barbed remarks to Daphnis in *Idyll I*.

Galatea . . . calls you a *duserōs* and a *goatherd*. (*VI* l. 7)
　　(Galatea to Polyphemus)
What a *duserōs* you are, and a fool.
Once you were called "the cowherd" but now you look
　　like a *goatherd*.
　　(*I* ll. 85 - 86) (Priapus to Daphnis)

Duserōs, as we have seen, means something on the order of "sexually neurotic," and "goatherd" is a professional insult, since neither
Polyphemus nor Daphnis herded goats.

The Polyphemus-Galatea myth in *Idyll VI* is as deliberately
obscure in its presentation as the myth of Daphnis in *Idyll I*.
Theocritus has intentionally left questions hanging. Why is the idyll
addressed to Aratus? What relationship can there be between a piping Cyclops and a passionate, teasing sea nymph? What does their
strange courtship mean? Theocritus gives us no direct clue as to the
meaning which the myth was meant to communicate; only in *Idyll
XI*, when he returns to his "fellow countryman" Polyphemus, does
he reveal the idea behind his personal version of the mythological
tale. In *Idyll VI* Theocritus leaves the reader free to interpret the
myth for himself. My own feeling is that a sentimentalizing or
trivializing interpretation is to be avoided. The Polyphemus-Galatea
myth enables Theocritus to evoke the eternal struggle of the poet
and his Muse in a humorous and ironic mode which avoids the ex-
tremes of pompous thematic amplification and sentimental triviali-
ty.

However, having just given the outlines of my own interpretation of the myth ("the eternal struggle of the poet and his muse"), I am perhaps justified in expressing a doubt as to the ultimate desirability of translating mythological terms into more modern analytical equivalents. Theocritus was a poet in whom the mythological sense had not atrophied, and for whom myths were elements of a more intuitive if less analytical and scientific language of the soul. It is one thing to claim, as I did, that Galatea is to be understood as an *anima* figure; it is quite another to assume that all has been explained by a simple switching of terms ((Nereid = Muse = *anima*). Jungian terminology is useful, in that it awakens in the modern reader a sense of the mysteriousness of human psychic life; but Jung himself had reservations about the use of scientific labels for their own sake:

The empirical reality summed up under the concept of the anima forms an extremely dramatic content of the unconscious. It is possible to describe this content in rational, scientific language, but in this way one entirely fails to express its living character. Therefore, in describing the living processes of the psyche, I deliberately and consciously give preference to a dramatic, mythological way of thinking and speaking. . . .[26]

In evoking the teasing game which Polyphemus and Galatea play, Theocritus has described in a "dramatic" and "mythological" way an "extremely dramatic content" of the poet's psychic and creative life. It is up to the reader not so much to interpret as to experience the myth through the poetry which serves as its vehicle of communication.

VI   Idyll VII *("The Harvest Festival")*

In *Idyll VII*, Simichidas, who is traveling with two friends from the city to a harvest festival in the countryside of the island of Cos, meets the goatherd Lycidas on the road at noon. Lycidas and Simichidas each sing a song, after which Lycidas gives his staff to Simichidas. The two part company, and Simichidas and his friends continue on their journey, and enjoy the harvest festival. The idyll consists of a narrative frame which leads up to the meeting with Lycidas (1 - 20) and ends with a short evocation of the harvest festival (127 - 57), and of a central portion, in which conversation between Lycidas and Simichidas (21 - 51, 90 - 95) alternates with the two songs (52 - 89, 96 - 27).

No other pastoral idyll of Theocritus has elicited more commentary and controversy.[27] Since space does not allow for a fair presentation of the various lines of interpretation which in recent years have increased our sense of the complexities of the text, I will attempt to discuss only those major elements in the poem which, in my opinion, need to be interpreted if the reader is to gain an adequate understanding of the poem as a whole as well as in its relation to the other pastoral idylls of Theocritus. These elements are the figures of Simichidas and Lycidas, the two songs, the staff which Lycidas gives to Simichidas, and the evocation of the harvest festival.

There is a consensus that *Idyll VII* is in some way or another an autobiographical poem, if only because the figure of Simichidas is often accepted as a mask for Theocritus himself. But there is no longer much interest in trying to unmask Lycidas, the most enigmatic figure of *Idyll VII*. He may represent one of the poets of Philetas' circle on Cos who enjoyed walking around disguised as a goatherd on occasion; this is the line of interpretation I followed in Chapter 1. But although it is possible that a poet disguised as a goatherd may have initially inspired Theocritus to create the figure of Lycidas, the figure as he is actually presented in *Idyll VII* is a three-dimensional fictional creation in his own right. Viewed from this perspective, Lycidas is neither a specific urban poet disguised as a goatherd, nor an àctual goatherd (where are his goats?), but a strongly individualized synthetic figure who combines the attributes of poet and goatherd in such a way as to preclude any breaking down of the herdsman-poet synthesis into its component parts. Lycidas is the perfect embodiment of the myth of the Theocritean Herdsman-Poet; yet unlike Daphnis, Comatas, or Polyphemus, he is not the hero of any particular mythological tale. He may well have some of the attributes of the satyrs of Alexandrian sculpture, as Lawall suggests;[28] but his quiet smile and ironic bantering with Simichidas establish him as thoroughly human. Lycidas is an intriguing figure, a mystery in broad daylight.

The song which Lycidas sings (52 - 89) at the urging of Simichidas is as intriguing and as enigmatic as the goatherd-poet himself. It starts out as a love song in honor of the boy Ageanax. Ageanax plans to leave Cos soon for Mitylene, and Lycidas is anxious to consummate the affair before his departure, because "the heat of his love is burning him to death" (52 - 62). Lycidas then imagines that Ageanax has granted his ardent requests, and has left Lycidas behind in Cos to remember him fondly. This strange nostalgia for what has yet to be leads Lycidas to imagine himself at a peculiar sort of private bucolic *symposion* or drinking party at which the goatherd himself is both host and the only guest, just after the departure of Ageanax for Mitylene. Lycidas sees himself reclining on a couch strewn with soft grasses, drinking wine and thinking of Ageanax with passionate gratitude. In a mood of increasing relaxation and contentment, Lycidas imagines two shepherds entertaining him with their piping (in an urban *symposion* there would be a flute girl or two, but Theocritus has Lycidas introduce the theme of bucolic music instead).

At this point, Lycidas' imagination begins to soar under the influence of the imagined music: Tityrus will sing to him the song about the sufferings of Daphnis, who loved the nymph Xenea only to waste away to the universal lament of Nature (72 - 77). This song suggests to Lycidas the idea for another song which Tityrus could sing to him—a song about Comatas (78 - 89), a goatherd-poet like himself (cf. *Idyll V*), who was locked up in a cedar chest on the order of a wicked king. But Comatas, unlike Daphnis, did *not* perish; the friendly bees, sensing the nectar which the Muses had poured on the poet's lips (82), came to his rescue and kept him alive with their honey. Lycidas is overcome by enthusiasm at the mythic power of this old story:

> O most blessed Comatas . . .
> if only you had been numbered among the living in my time;
> for then I could have herded your lovely goats on the slopes
> while I listened to your voice, and you under oaks or under pines
> would have reclined and made sweet music, o divine Comatas!
> (ll. 83, 86 - 89)

The sequential arrangement of the motifs of this song is quite strange, if one looks at it closely; Gow finds it "puzzling." Lycidas does indeed have a sophisticated and ever-shifting imagination. In this eminently poetic fantasy, he is able to anticipate his gratitude to Ageanax, his passionate remembrance and his commemorative celebration of a love which he has not even enjoyed as yet, and which he has entirely forgotten by the end of the song in his enthusiasm for the songs of a poet he has never heard! This astonishing flight of his poetic imagination is positively dizzying.

On second glance, it becomes clear that this flight of the imagination is spurred on by the theme of sublimation. The poem begins with sexual desire for a boy, and ends with an aesthetic longing for the presence of the blessed archpoet Comatas. By the end of his song Lycidas has forgotten Ageanax; he ends his song in a kind of ecstasy, as he imagines himself listening to sweet music in a pastoral poet's Elysium.

In Lycidas' song, the myth of Comatas (78 - 89) is introduced right after Tityrus has sung of the sufferings of Daphnis (72 - 77). The myth of Comatas and the myth of Daphnis belong together, since each deals with the unusual sufferings inflicted on a herdsman-poet. But if the myth of Daphnis is tragic, the myth of Comatas at least has a happy ending: Comatas miraculously escapes death, and, thanks to the bees, survives to sing again in the shade. His fate is not to experience *algea* ("sufferings"), as Daphnis did, but *terpna* (84, "delights")—there may be some irony in the expression (being locked up in a coffer was not in itself delightful), but the term chosen by Lycidas certainly indicates the happy outcome of what could have been a tragic and slow death by starvation.

Why did Daphnis waste away, whereas Comatas survived? The easiest answer, which the song itself suggests, is that the Muse's nectar on the lips of Comatas saved his life, since it attracted the bees who fed him; whereas Daphnis was abandoned by the nymphs in his hour of need. In less mythological terms, poetry enabled Comatas to survive, just as his song enables Lycidas to forget the heat of his passion for Ageanax.

The song (96 - 127) which Simichidas sings in reply to Lycidas' song, is a more prosaic commentary on the same theme of how to cope with a desperate passion. Simichidas' friend Aratus, like Lycidas, is in love with a boy. This boy's name is Philinus; and he, like Ageanax, has not yet given in to his lover's demands; thus Aratus, like Lycidas, is burning with unsatisfied desire (cf. lines 56 and 102, where the same metaphors of love and fire are used). The theme of the song then shifts to a plea to the god Pan, whose divine intervention is needed to bring the reluctant Philinus into the arms of Aratus. The amusingly bizarre description of the Arcadian ritual flogging of the statue of Pan (106 - 14) adds a note of bucolic fantasy which corresponds to the fantastic *symposion* which Lycidas arranges for himself; in both cases, the extravagance of the description transforms the symposiastic theme[29] of unsatisfied desire into a pastoral theme whose humor and oddness distract the mind from the actual problems of sexual frustration. Simichidas' song returns to the theme of unrequited love at the end (121 - 27)—but only in order to urge Aratus to forget about Philinus, and to cultivate peace of mind (*hasuchia*—see Chapter 1, section III) instead of passion.

Although the songs of Lycidas and Simichidas are similar from the standpoint of theme and structure, the mode of expression is different in each case. In Lycidas' song, an intriguing evocation of the myth of Comatas is used in order to clear away the passionate and nostalgic notes of the earlier part of the song, and to substitute for the image of an amorous Lycidas an ecstatic Lycidas who listens with rapt attention to the songs of a bucolic archpoet. In Simichidas' more urban and more Alexandrian song, the exhortation to his friend Aratus to forget his passion for Philinus is based on an appeal to reason and to the Epicurean ideal of *hasuchia*. In other words, the mode of expression in Lycidas' song is primarily *mythic*, whereas it is *conceptual* in Simichidas' reply. The difference between these two modes of expression results from what John Finley has called the "revolution" in Greek thought "by which conceptual thinking replaced the old reliance on myth."[30]

The encounter between Lycidas and Simichidas is thus symbolic of the encounter between the old world of myth represented by the goatherd Lycidas, and the new world of Epicurean rationalism represented by the poet himself. The staff which Lycidas gives to Simichidas as a gift of friendship between fellow poets (129 *ek Moisan xeineion*) represents the link which Theocritus' bucolic poetry established between the older tradition of poetic myth and the new world of the *oikoumenē* where conceptual habits of thought were rapidly reducing myth to the level of a pedant's game. It was by reestablishing the connection with the great tradition of mythic discourse that Theocritus was able to give to Greek literature its last poetic masterpiece, the *Pastoral Idylls*.

Idyll VII contains numerous references to the Muses and the Nymphs (cf. 12, 37, 47, 59, 82, 92, 95, 129, 137, 148, 154), by means of which Theocritus is able to introduce the theme of poetry allegorically and provide a proper thematic context for the meeting of Simichidas and Lycidas, which is, after all, a meeting of poets as well as of poetic traditions. These references foreshadow the peculiar way in which the harvest festival is described at the end of *Idyll VII* (132 - 57). The festival evokes the atmosphere of rural abundance which we would expect in such a description: "all things smelled of grain and fruit harvested in abundance" (143). But of the actual festival itself there is practically nothing said. In fact, what is described is more reminiscent of a sacred enclosure where water splashes from the cave of the Nymphs (134 - 35), and where the Castalian Nymphs pour nectar (153), the divine drink of the gods, for the invited guests (148 - 54). Nectar is a word associated with poetry in *Idyll VII*, since the Muse had poured nectar on the lips of the bucolic archpoet Comatas (82); and water, all the more if it flowed from the cave of the Nymphs (134 - 35), had a traditional association with poetry and creative inspiration. The *locus amoenus* at the end of *Idyll VII* is typically Theocritean, in that it associates pastoral motifs with the theme of poetry.

At the center of this *locus amoenus* stands the altar of Demeter (155), the goddess who is being honored at this harvest festival and whose name is mentioned three times in the course of *Idyll VII* (3, 32, 155). It is the smile of Demeter which is the last image of the idyll (154). Her smile is kind, not like the crafty smile of Aphrodite in *Idyll I* (cf. *I* ll. 95 - 96); perhaps Lycidas, who was always smiling and laughing gently (cf. 20, 42, 128: *gelan* means both "to smile" and "to laugh" in Greek), got his smile from her. Demeter is a kind mother goddess, so different from the jealous goddess of Love who persecuted Daphnis. Demeter's smile blesses Simichidas-Theocritus after his encounter with the goatherd poet, when the staff was given to him as a sign that now he was worthy to be called a bucolic poet. The Great Mother, who brings disaster to lovers, is kind and propitious to poets.

Idyll VII is the most illuminating "portrait of the artist" which Theocritus has left of himself. It is certainly autobiographic, although far more in the inner than in the outer sense. The journey to the harvest festival and the meeting with Lycidas reflect in symbolic fashion the most important event of the life of Theocritus, that is, the moment when his rationalistic and Epicurean temperament (Simichidas) awakened to poetry and to the mythic sense of life.

VII   The Eleventh Idyll

In *Idyll XI* the Cyclops Polyphemus sings a song which, according to Theocritus, cures him of the suffering caused by his unrequited love for the sea nymph Galatea. The idyll consists of a narrative frame (1 - 18, 80 - 81), in which Theocritus tells his doctor friend Nicias that only the Muses can provide a remedy for love (1 - 6), as the myth of Polyphemus illustrates (7 - 18); and of

Polyphemus' song, which takes the form of a lyric monologue (19 - 79).

The frame of *Idyll XI* is unusual, since, in contrast to his practice in the other *Pastoral Idylls* Theocritus appears *in propria persona*, and addresses Nicias in his own voice. Of course, the figure of Simichidas represented Theocritus under the flimsiest of pastoral disguises in *Idyll VII*, and *Idyll VI* is also addressed to a friend, Aratus, although without explanation, as we have seen. In *Idyll XI*, the frame introduces both an idea and a myth through the direct voice of the poet:

> There is no cure for love, Nicias; nothing helps
> —no ointment, I fear, not even a plaster—
> except the Pierian Muses. Ah—how painless and sweet
> *this* cure is for mortals; if only they can find it.
> (And well you should know, for you are a doctor
> and the special beloved of all the nine Muses.)
> And that is why all went well with my fellow Sicilian,
> the Cyclops Polyphemus, when he loved Galatea.
>   (ll. 1 - 8)

It is thus the idea that "only the Muses can cure the disease of love" which becomes the motivating idea of the idyll as a whole.

Greek medicine was not unaware of the possible therapeutic effects of music and poetry, and Aristotle in the *Politics* (VIII l.7) had listed among the three effects of music its capacity to purify the passions, that is, to bring about a *katharsis* of the emotions and thus reestablish an emotional equilibrium in an agitated mind. Theocritus' friend Nicias, who was a poet as well as a doctor (5 - 6), should not have found the idea of *Idyll XI* hard to grasp, although modern commentators have only recently taken it seriously.[31] However, the idea is a subtle one, since it implies that the Cyclops found in the act of creating verse a deliberately chosen means to sublimate his excess of sexual energy. It is true that other protagonists of the *Pastoral Idylls* such as Comatas in *Idyll V* and Lycidas in *Idyll VII* literally sang themselves into a less passionate and more peaceful frame of mind; but the theme of poetry as sublimation is perhaps easier to communiate than the idea itself.

It is ironic that Nicias may have been the first to fail to catch the full import of the advice which Theocritus had addressed to him. A scholiast has preserved a fragment attributed to the doctor, no doubt part of a longer reply to *Idyll XI:*

Yes, there we have the plain truth, Theocritus:
Love has made poets out of many formerly museless men.

As Gow has correctly pointed out, Nicias' two lines of verse make little sense in the context of the frame of *Idyll XI*, and are in all events a paraphrase of Euripides.[32] One hopes that Nicias had more to say than that.

A much more appropriate response to the idea of *Idyll XI* has survived in the forty-seventh epigram of Callimachus, the illustrious Alexandrian contemporary of Theocritus. Coming from a poet of genuine ability, this intelligent and witty appreciation is most welcome:

What a good spell Polyphemus found for lovers!
    By Earth, that Cyclops was no dunce!
The Muses take the swelling out of Love—
    our poet's craft cures everything!

Callimachus has tightened up the analogy from medicine which Theocritus introduced and describes the Cyclops' song and poetry in general as a verbal healing spell *(epaoida)*, although he also uses the more general term "remedy" or "cure" *(pharmakon)* which Theocritus used (cf. line 4 of Callimachus' epigram and *Idyll XI* l. 1). In lines 5 and 6 of this epigram, however, Callimachus develops an original variation on the Theocritean theme of a cure for love: he suggests, tongue in cheek, that hunger can also cure poets of the disease of chasing after young boys *(tan philopaida noson)*, and that poets are thus doubly protected against the onslaughts of fierce desire, whether they starve, or whether they versify. Callimachus has cleverly reduced the rather exalted idea of *Idyll XI* to a question of mere physiology: an empty stomach chases away thoughts of love.

Theocritus obviously considers the Cyclops' passion to be a dangerous state of mind which needs to be "cured." This is not surprising, since he felt much the same way about Aratus' passion for Philinus in *Idyll VII*. Theocritus' intellectual position on sexual passion was Epicurean, as we have already noted (Chapter 1, section III): "the Epicureans do not suffer a wise man to fall in love."[33]

And Polyphemus was definitely in love with Galatea, even to the point of near insanity: he loved her "not with apples" and the usual love tokens, but presented her, as it were, with "downright fits of madness" (11) as tokens of his affection.

The state of mind of Polyphemus in this first phase of his love for Galatea (8 - 16) is a dangerous one, because it brings to mind the tragic myth of Daphnis. When Polyphemus was in love with Galatea, he began to "waste away" as Daphnis did in *Idyll I*. We have already noted several parallels between the myths of Daphnis and Polyphemus; a disturbing use of the verb *katetaketo* (wasted away) should be noted as well, since in *Idyll XI* l. 14, where it refers to Polyphemus, it occupies the same metrical position as in *Idyll VII* l. 76, where it refers to Daphnis and his approaching death (cf. also *Idyll I* ll. 66, 82). Thus Polyphemus, "when he loved Galatea" (8), is disturbingly reminiscent of Daphnis, "when he was in love with Xenea" (*Idyll VII* l. 73). If we read lines 13 - 16 with an eye for the original violence of what has become metaphorical language, it is clear that Aphrodite has attempted to find the same kind of victim in Polyphemus that she found in Daphnis, and that the Cyclops' very life is in peril:

> Polyphemus, singing of Galatea,
> wasted away on the seaweed-covered beach
> from dawn to dusk; for he had a terrible wound which
> Aphrodite the great goddess had opened with a bolt to his liver.

Greek medicine considered the liver to be the seat of the passions. The language of this description, however metaphorical in extension, bodes ill for the Cyclops' survival, since Aphrodite is no mere modern Valentine Cupid, but the Great Goddess who comes to watch Daphnis die in *Idyll I*.

From line 17 on in *Idyll XI*, the Theocritean myth of Polyphemus, which hitherto ran parallel to the myth of Daphnis (a herdsman-poet falls in love and begins to waste away), suddenly starts out in a new direction:

> But as for the remedy, he found it; and sitting
> high up on a rock, looked seawards and sang the following song. . . .
> (17 - 18)

With the lines just quoted, the scene changes slightly, and the

drama takes a new turn. The song which Polyphemus is now about
to sing is clearly different in nature from the song which he was
singing before. His first song brought him no relief as he wasted
away on the beach "singing of Galatea" (13); his second song is the
remedy (*pharmakon*) which, as Theocritus tells Nicias, is the only
cure for love. The difference between the two types of singing is
marked by the change in the location of the singer: Polyphemus
sang his first song down below on the beach (14), but the second
and, therapeutically speaking, *decisive* song he sings from a high
rock overlooking the sea; it is a song sung on a hill, that is, a
pastoral song. This pastoral song is no mere lover's lament, but
rather a conscious summoning and activation through song of the
creative powers of erotic sublimation. The Cyclops sings in order to
cure his dangerously depressed state of mind, not in order to woo
Galatea.

The result of the Cyclops' singing was that "he got along quite
well" (*raista diag'* 7, cf. 81); the point is such an important one that
Theocritus repeats it at the end of the idyll, when he closes the
frame:

> Well, this is the way Polyphemus shepherded his love
> by making music, and got on better than if he had paid gold
>   [to a doctor].
>   (ll. 80 - 81)

The expression "shepherded his love/by making music"
(*epoimainen ton erōta/mousisdōn* 80 - 81) is original and quite apt.
To "shepherd" love suggests that Polyphemus took care of the
amorous preoccupations of his mind as carefully as a good shepherd
like himself would take care of his sheep; the latent sexual symbolism of livestock in the *Pastoral Idylls* surfaces again. I am
reminded of a line of Sir Philip Sidney from "Dorus His Comparisons": "My sheep are thoughts, which I both guide and serve,"
where the allegory is made explicit. In Theocritus' line 80, the par-
ticiple *mousisdon* is a terse reminder that only through the Muses
(cf. 3) is a cure for love to be found, a better one than doctors could
be paid to provide. Thus we are to imagine the Cyclops at the end
of his song to have fallen out of love with Galatea, at least to the extent of having reduced his passion for her to manageable proportions. In Aristotelian terms, Polyphemus has experienced a comic
catharsis of his erotic feelings for Galatea, and this purification or

purgation through song has reduced these emotions to more healthy proportions, leaving Polyphemus his old carefree self again.

The song which Polyphemus sings (19 - 79) contains several comic motifs which were much imitated by later pastoral poets.[34] Polyphemus praises Galatea with country comparisons (20 - 21); he recalls the flower-gathering expedition when he first fell in love with her (25 - 27); he boasts of his wealth in cattle and cheese (34 - 37); he praises his own skill in piping and singing (38 - 40); he offers the nymph rather outlandish presents (eleven fawns and four bear cubs, 40 - 41), and begs her to leave the sea and come live with him in his pastoral paradise (42 - 49, 63 - 66).

The ridiculous posturings of the Cyclops and the comic motifs of his song hardly lead us to expect that he seriously intends Galatea to listen to his complaint. The tone of *Idyll III*, where we find a similarly inept love song, is clearly bathetic, whereas the tone of *Idyll XI* is comic and ironic. In other words, the silly goatherd of *Idyll III* took himself and his love for Amaryllis all too seriously, whereas Polyphemus is making fun of himself and of his impossible love for an elusive Nereid in *Idyll XI*.

The Cyclops' self-mockery and the ironic tone of the song prepare the way for the sudden reversal of the situation in lines 72 - 79. Like the silly goatherd's serenade in *Idyll III*, the Cyclops' lament ends, ridiculously, when he complains of having a headache (cf. *III* l. 52 and *XI* ll. 70 - 71). However, unlike the goatherd in *Idyll III*, the Cyclops does not continue his attempts to elicit some sign of compassion from his reluctant nymph, but rather gives himself the pastoral equivalent of the sort of Epicurean advice which Theocritus was wont to give his friends (72 - 79):

Ah, Cyclops, Cyclops, have you lost all your wits?
Go and weave some cheese crates, gather greenery
and bring it to your lambs—that would be more sensible.
Milk the ewe at hand; why chase after one that runs away?
You'll probably find another Galatea, and a prettier one too.
Lots of girls ask me to play games with them at night,
And all of them giggle, when they know I'm listening.
It's a fact that, on land, I too amount to something.

At the equivalent point in *Idyll III*, the silly goatherd was lying down to wait for the wolves to come and eat him. Polyphemus, however, has cured himself of his obsession with the image of the lovely Galatea.

In turning to the giggling Sicilian girls of line 78, Polyphemus is acting as an Epicurean, not a romantic, herdsman-poet; better to be unfaithful to the beloved than to lose one's wits over a dream. The Roman Epicurean poet Lucretius was later to give similar advice to the young lover who found himself plagued and obsessed with the insubstantial image (*simulacrum*) of the absent object of his desires, in a passage from *On the Nature of Things (De Rerum Natura)* where Epicurean physics joins with Epicurean psychology. Lucretius had this to say (*IV* ll. 1063 - 67):

> One must flee from such insubstantial images, avoid
> giving sustenance to one's passion, turn one's mind to
>   other objects of desire,
> and ejaculate into the first available body,
> rather than to hold back the sperm for the sake of a
>   single beloved,
> and thus deliberately cause oneself mental distress and
>   physical pain.

But the Lucretian analogy is not a perfect one, since Galatea is no ordinary girl. In *Idyll XI* we never even get a glimpse of Galatea, nor does Polyphemus: Galatea appears only in his dreams (22 - 24). It is true that Polyphemus associates Galatea with the memory of some childhood girl friend with whom he went on a flower-gathering expedition; but the sea nymph who in both *Idylls VI* and *XI* never leaves the waves of the Mediterranean can hardly be imagined gathering hyacinths on the hill (25 - 27). Galatea is thus presented in *Idyll XI* as an elusive insubstantial image compounded of dream and memory elements; she is, to that extent, an imaginary being, although she has all the psychic reality of a Jungian *anima* figure (cf. the discussion of *Idyll VI* in this chapter). Clearly the land-bound Cyclops and the sea-dwelling Nereid are players in an elemental comedy of basic incompatibility, where sea and land, dream and reality, can hardly be expected to achieve anything beyond an imaginary reconciliation.

Thus Polyphemus is not actually plagued by the image or *simulacrum* of the "real" Galatea; rather, Galatea *is* that imaginary, insubstantial image. Appropriately enough, the Cyclops cures himself of his obsession with Galatea through an act of the imagination; that is, he sings himself into a state of reasonable content with himself and his pastoral life. Ovid's *Remedia Amoris*, whose very title ("The Cures for Love," *remedium* being the Latin equivalent of the Greek *pharmakon* of *XI* l. 1) reminds us of the opening of *Idyll XI*, offers a more pertinent analogue. "Learn how to cure yourself of Love from the same poet who taught you to love in the first place *(Discite sanari, per quem didicisti amare)*, exclaimed the author of *The Art of Love*, proud that he could teach both arts. Among the many cures for love which Ovid urged on unhappy lovers, one at least places particular emphasis on the therapeutic powers of the imagination (ll. 497, 504):

Feign what is not, and make a good show of passionless calm.
He who can *pretend* that he is cured, soon will *be* cured.

This is certainly close to the procedure which the Cyclops follows at the end of his song.

But *Idyll XI* does more than urge Epicurean abstention from passionate entanglements. The motivating idea that "poetry cures love" restates the theme of the creative sublimation of sexual desire which is so important in the *Pastoral Idylls*. *Idyll XI* also presents the Theocritean myth of Polyphemus and Galatea in a new light. In *Idyll VI*, Polyphemus piped away on his syrinx as he feigned indifference to Galatea's charms; in *Idyll XI* he sings, that is, he creates poetry, which, as in *Idyll I*, is a more sophisticated bucolic form of artistic creativity. By singing, he is able, like Lycidas in *Idyll VII* and Comatas in *Idyll V*, to take his mind off of the object of his passionate obsession and attain that "peace of mind" *(hasychia)* which Theocritus championed. Seen from this Theocritean perspective, the young Polyphemus is emblematic of the power of art to change an unhappy state of mind into a happy one. His poetic activity constitutes a partial sublimation of the sexual instincts, in that it directs (or "shepherds") sexual energy into poetic activity of a comic-bucolic variety. In *Idyll XI* Polyphemus is brought to a point where he takes himself less seriously as a lover, and more seriously as a poet.

The frame of *Idyll XI* contains a theme which is not illustrated by the song which it introduces: the theme of pastoral friendship.[35] The opening lines of the poem are no mere formal dedication. Although we cannot be sure that Nicias was in love at the time, or that he stood in specific need of the advice which Theocritus had to give him, nevertheless the whole of *Idyll XI* may be read as a message of consolation from one friend to another who is suffering

from the disease of love. This theme of consolation is just as important as the theme of a cure for love through poetry, from which it
may be said to derive. If poetry is a cure for love, this cure does not
leave the poet in the happy state of narcissistic isolation which
Polyphemus enjoys at the end of his song. Through poetry this state
of isolation, self-induced through the Cyclops' initial desire to brood
over his unhappy love, is transcended; and Polyphemus is brought
into the circle of poets, poets such as Theocritus and Nicias, whose
warmth of mutual appreciation and whose Epicurean friendship are
celebrated in practically every one of the bucolic idylls of
Theocritus.

VIII   *The* Pastoral Idylls *as a Poetic Sequence*

Nothing in the manuscript tradition enables us to claim that
Theocritus arranged his *Pastoral Idylls* in a particular sequence. The
numbering of the idylls is the result of a process of editing which,
although it dates back to antiquity, cannot be considered as
necessarily reflecting any arrangement which Theocritus may have
intended.[36] Until the sands of Egypt yield up a "poetry book" of the
sort Lawall has suggested was the form in which the *Pastoral Idylls*
were first published, any consideration of them as forming a poetic
sequence rests on strictly interpretive grounds.

Modern commentators have at least two advantages over their
predecessors. First of all, we are almost certain that *Idylls VIII* and
IX are *not* by Theocritus, and that they are thus not parts of any
book of pastoral poetry which Theocritus may have published.
Secondly, modern notions of generic criteria are different from and,
I would say, superior to, those of ancient editors, whose heavy
reliance on metrics and dialect seems quite arbitrary by modern
standards.

I take it as axiomatic that the presence of the Herdsman-Poet
protagonist is as essential to Theocritean pastoral as a tragic hero is
to Greek tragedy. Since the only idylls where such protagonists
appear are *Idylls I, III - VII,* and *XI*, these should be considered as
the only genuinely pastoral idylls which can be credited to
Theocritus. Whether these pastoral idylls form a group, and
whether they form a poetic sequence when read in the order in
which they are listed above, are two questions which I shall now
attempt to answer.

Is it likely that Theocritus wrote each pastoral idyll with little or no concern for its relation to, or place in, a group of *Pastoral Idylls?* Or is it more likely that, somewhere along the line between conception and final revision for publication, Theocritus saw his poems as constituting a collection or "poetry book"? Gilbert Lawall sees in *Idyll VII* the ultimate sanction for the assumption of the existence of a book of "Coan Idylls": "the hypothesis of a Coan collection is new to Theocritean scholarship, and somewhat surprisingly so, for the seventh idyll virtually demands such an assumption."[37] Lawall's interpretation of *Idyll VII* as "a pastiche, an elaborate transferal, adaptation, and regrouping of the language, places, characters, literary forms, and dramatic situations of the Coan Idylls," and as "a recapitulation of the entire poetry book,"[38] is ingenious, although I feel that he places too much emphasis on what he considers to be the unique position of *Idyll VII* in the collection. There is a complex network of relationships which binds *Idylls I, III - VII,* and *XI* together. Lawall's hypothesis has two basic flaws: it groups *Idyll II* with the pastoral idylls, for reasons which I do not find convincing, and it omits *Idyll XI* from consideration. Otherwise, it is a most useful hypothesis, with which I am thoroughly in agreement: the *Pastoral Idylls* form a collection.

One rather obvious argument for considering the *Pastoral Idylls* as a group (although not yet as a sequence, which is another matter), is the constant reappearance of the same pastoral protagonists: Daphnis in *Idyll I,* then in *Idyll VI;* Amaryllis in *Idyll III,* then in *Idyll IV,* and so on. Actually, the issue is not so simple. Is the Amaryllis who lives in the cave in *Idyll III* the same Amaryllis to whom the athlete Aegon gave a bull in Corydon's song in *Idyll IV* ll. 35 - 37? Is the boisterous Comatas of *Idyll V* to be identified with the "divine" Comatas of Lycidas' song in *Idyll VII?* Such are the problems we face when we attempt to view the *Pastoral Idylls* as a bucolic *Comédie Humaine* where familiar characters pop up unexpectedly. But the weight of the evidence is rather overwhelming, and there is enough consistency in Theocritus' naming of his pastoral protagonists to enable us to conclude that Theocritus never repeats a pastoral name carelessly or without definite intention, however difficult that intention may be for us to discover. The attempt is certainly worth making.

Thus it is clear that the Corydon whom Comatas calls, in *Idyll V* ll. 6 - 7, an insignificant fellow who, for want of a syrinx, plays on a simple reed whistle, is the same Corydon who, in *Idyll IV* ll. 29 - 30, is made so cheerful by Aegon's gift of a syrinx. The Daphnis of *Idyll*

VI is most certainly to be identified with the Daphnis of *Idyll I*, for reasons we have discussed already; and it is certainly his sad story which is alluded to by both Lacon and Comatas in *Idyll V* (20, 80 - 81), and which is summarized in Lycidas' song in *Idyll VII* ll. 72 - 77. Why Amaryllis should be mentioned in both *Idylls III* and *IV* remains a mystery to me, but there surely is some reason behind the exact repetition "o lovely Amaryllis" in *III* l. 6 and *IV* l. 38 (see my discussion of *Idyll IV*). The friendly Tityrus who herds goats in *Idyll III* ll. 2 - 5 entertains Lycidas with his songs in *Idyll VII* ll. 72 - 82; and the silly goatherd of *Idyll III* shares a certain naïveté with his equally nameless counterpart in the frame of *Idyll I*, with whom he might as well be identified, although in *Idyll III* he is no doubt younger and more foolish. Two versions of the myth of Polyphemus and Galatea are given in *Idylls VI* and *XI;* although the Cyclops of *VI* is a piper and the other a singer as well, both love Galatea, whose elusive beauty is viewed from two different perspectives: in *VI* she is a teasing Nymph who throws apples like the Clearista of *Idyll V*, and in *XI* she is a reluctant and invisible Nymph like Amaryllis in *Idyll III*. There is no reason not to identify the talented and foul-smelling Comatas of *Idyll V* with the mythic Comatas of *Idyll VII*, since Lycidas' imagination has simply idealized the image of the long dead goatherd poet who is so very much alive in his altercation with Lacon. Aside from these strictly fictional creations, Theocritus' friend Aratus is addressed in *Idyll VI* l. 2, and is the subject of a song in *Idyll VII*. And finally, Theocritus himself, who appears only lightly disguised as Simichidas in *Idyll VII*, speaks in his own voice in the frame of *Idyll XI*.

Given the fact that Theocritus distributed a small cast of characters among his various pastoral idylls, it would be strange indeed if the poet had not intended us to consider the *Pastoral Idylls* as a group. It remains to be seen, however, whether the *Pastoral Idylls* constitute a collection of loosely related poems[39] or whether they form a poetic *sequence*—that is, a fixed arrangement of poems where a definite order is followed in the interests of thematic development, whose unity transcends the unity of the individual pieces which compose it.

Throughout my discussion of the individual pastoral idylls, I have assumed that it is frequently possible to interpret one poem in the light of another, and my comments have reflected that assumption. But I am also of the opinion that *Idylls I, III - VII*, and *XI*, read in that order, further the aims of a thematic development which any other arrangement (and I can imagine several interesting ones) would fail to communicate. Each poem, for all that it constitutes a unity of its own, slowly advances the progress of a poetic drama. Each poem adds another dimension to the Theocritean vision of life which it both enriches and clarifies. Each poem is brought into existence by the combined poetic impulses of the preceding poems, and each prepares the way for the final resolution of those impulses. For all their variety of themes, motifs, protagonists, etc., the seven *Pastoral Idylls* are linked together like the acts of a play.

However, there exists no definite proof that Theocritus wrote his *Pastoral Idylls* as a poetic sequence, or even that he necessarily arranged them in such a sequence for publication and revised them accordingly, although I would favor this second hypothesis. Although the Vatican manuscript tradition could be said to favor the *I, III - VII* and *XI* order (once the spurious or nonpastoral idylls—*VIII, IX, II,* and *X*—have been removed from the sequence), this particular arrangement could have just as easily been the creation of an early editor of the *Idylls*. Nevertheless, once it appears likely that Theocritus deliberately encouraged the reader to view the *Pastoral Idylls* as a collection, it is natural to assume that he had them published in a particular order as well, an order which reflected a concern for the greater thematic unity of the collection. And if the *Pastoral Idylls* were intended to be read in any sequence at all, there are several good reasons for ordering that sequence in the way I have suggested.

There are three major Theocritean myths in the *Pastoral Idylls:* the myths of Daphnis *(Idyll I)*, Comatas *(Idyll VII)*, and Polyphemus *(Idyll XI)*. Although the bucolic vision is basically a comic one, the myth of Daphnis, in spite of comic elements (the teasing and taunting of Daphnis), is a tragic myth. The myth of Polyphemus is, as we have seen, its comic counterpart: Daphnis dies of love, the Cyclops cures himself of his erotic depression and does *not* waste away. The myth of Comatas as presented by Lycidas in *Idyll VII* tells of the miraculous deliverance of a poet from certain death, but it lacks the theme of desperate passion. These three myths stand in a dialectical relationship, which can be expressed most simply as follows:

Daphnis *(I)* loves and dies.   (thesis)
Comatas *(VII)* survives.   (antithesis)
Polyphemus *(XI)* loves and survives.   (synthesis)

The three scenes on the cup in *Idyll I* ll. 32 - 54 were presented in dialectical sequence, and a dialectical ordering for these myths would establish the sequence of *Idylls I, VII,* and *XI.*

In the seven *Pastoral Idylls,* each of the three main mythic protagonists is introduced twice (casual references aside): Daphnis in *Idylls I* and *VI,* Comatas in *Idylls V* and *VII,* and Polyphemus in *Idylls VI* and *XI.* However, the Daphnis and the Polyphemus of *VI,* as well as the Comatas of *V,* are presented without direct reference to the particular Theocritean myth with which they are associated in *Idylls I, XI,* and *VII;* although the Cyclops in *Idyll VI* is feigning indifference to Galatea, he has not yet assumed the mythic role of the one who cures himself of love through singing. In other words, each of the three figures appears once in his major mythic role, and once in a more or less demythologized form as simple herdsman-poet.

The myth of Daphnis is introduced by the shepherd Thyrsis in *Idyll I,* the myth of Comatas by Lycidas in *VII,* and the myth of Polyphemus by Theocritus himself in *XI.* The literary status of the introducer corresponds to the dialectical importance of the myth: Thyrsis is presented as an actual rural singer, Lycidas as a figure combining the attributes of goatherd and urban poet, and Theocritus, in the frame of *Idyll XI,* speaks with the undisguised voice of the poet.

Idyll XI illustrates through the myth of Polyphemus the idea that poetry is the solution to the problem of love, and this idea may be seen as the conceptual expression of the theme of creative sublimation which surfaces in *Idyll V,* although it is latent in the earlier pastoral idylls. Since most of the pastoral protagonists of the *Pastoral Idylls* are lovers as well as poets, the sequence *I, III - VII,* and *XI* may be read as a poetic drama, in which the Herdsman-Poet, appearing in various forms, manifests an increasing ability to counter erotic frustration with creative activity. Daphnis in *Idyll I* represents the Herdsman-Poet completely vanquished by love. The silly goatherd of *Idyll III,* although his passion for Amaryllis overwhelms him and his poetry is ridiculous, nevertheless is one step removed from the passivity and tragic silence of "the sufferings of Daphnis." Corydon in *Idyll IV* cheers up Battus with his snatches of song, and Comatas in *Idyll V* is a master of creative sublimation in his own crude way. In *Idyll VI* Daphnis and Damoetas express their friendly feelings towards each other through song, and a cheerful Daphnis introduces the first version of the comic myth of

Polyphemus. *Idylls VII* and *XI* are quite similar in their treatment of the themes of love and poetry, and the song of Lycidas is the prelude to the song of Polyphemus and the motivating idea behind it, which makes conceptually explicit in *Idyll XI* what was thematically explicit in *Idyll VII*. Both Lycidas and Polyphemus provide the strongest possible contrast with the lovelorn Daphnis and with the overly serious goatherd lover of Amaryllis in the first two pastoral idylls.

As the theme of the power of poetry as creative sublimation comes to the fore, it is interesting to note how the Herdsman-Poet, the collective hero of the *Pastoral Idylls*, becomes not only less of a lover and more of a poet, but also less of a herdsman and more of a poet. The contrast between the goatherd Comatas of *Idyll V* and the goatherd Lycidas of *Idyll VII* indicates such a shift. Comatas is boisterous and crude, definitely the lower-class herdsman in his ways, and his amoebaean singing match with Lacon is partially modelled on actual herdsmen's singing, as we have seen. Lycidas, although he wears a smelly goatskin (*VII* ll. 15 - 16, cf. V ll. 51 - 52), is quite a sophisticated poet, whose ironic mannerisms hardly suit his role as an uneducated rustic. In the first half or so of the *Pastoral Idylls*, we are mainly presented with the Herdsman-Poet in full pastoral dress and regalia; in the second half, the disguise falls away to reveal the Poet. The most extreme contrast would be between the nameless goatherds of *Idylls I* and *III*, and the lightly disguised Theocritus-Simichidas of *Idyll VII* and the Theocritus *in propria persona* of the frame of *Idyll XI*. Theocritus' own circle of friends and fellow poets emerges, first with a mere mention of the name of Aratus in *Idyll VI* l. 2, and then more fully in *Idyll VII* and the frame of *Idyll XI*. This pattern of increasing the protagonists' ability as poets from one idyll to the next explains, for example, the way Corydon is presented in *Idyll IV* as opposed to *Idyll V*. In *Idyll IV*, Corydon has all the makings of pastoral mythmaker and singer (cf. *IV* ll. 29 - 37); but for the more vigorously creative Comatas of *Idyll V*, Corydon is a simple rustic who pipes away on a reed (V ll. 6 - 7).

The drama of the Herdsman-Poet opens in *Idyll I* with a question: "Where were you, Nymphs, when Daphnis was wasting away?" (*I* l. 66). Throughout the remaining pastoral idylls, the sequence develops a reply to Thyrsis' anguished question. The theme of creative sublimation increasingly dominates the theme of lovelorn despair and "the sufferings of Daphnis," until in *Idyll V* the goatherd Comatas can sing that "the Muses love me far more than the singer Daphnis" (V l. 80). Damoetas answers Daphnis' puzzled question about the attitude of Polyphemus towards the teasing Galatea in *Idyll VI*, and in *Idyll VII* the myth of Daphnis is countered with the myth of Comatas (*VII* ll. 78 - 89). At last in *Idyll XI* ll. 1 - 3 an answer is given to the question raised by the myth of Daphnis who suffered so terribly when he loved Xenea: "only the Muses can cure the sufferings of love."

To suggest that the *Pastoral Idylls* can be read as a sequence is not to rule out other readings, as long as these readings can account for the network of themes and motifs which bind the poems together. It is possible to view a statue from a number of interesting angles, and viewing the *Pastoral Idylls* as a dramatic sequence is only one possible way of coming to terms with the existence of a number of thematic concerns which are developed from idyll to idyll. Each individual pastoral idyll also has a dramatic structure of its own, and thus deserves to be considered as a separate entity.

I doubt if the individual pastoral idylls were first written in view of any sequential arrangement. To my mind, the most reasonable hypothesis would be that the *Pastoral Idylls* (unlike Virgil's *Eclogues*) were first written as individual pieces, and only later were revised for publication at a time when Theocritus desired to tighten the poetic threads which already bound one pastoral idyll to another, and to make use of the Daphnis-Polyphemus polarity, whose tension made possible a more dramatic presentation of his collection of pastoral poems.

CHAPTER 3

The Other Poems

" "THO Theocritus passes in common Esteem for no more than a Pastoral Poet, yet he is manifestly robb'd of a great part of his Fame if his other Pieces have not their proper Laurels." Thus wrote Basil Kennet, author of the first English life of Theocritus, in *Lives and Characters of the Ancient Grecian Poets* (1697), and I see no reason to modify his statement. Several of the nonpastoral poems of Theocritus are as beautiful and as interesting as any of the pastoral idylls, even though they have not had the same influence on the course of Western literature. If only the nonpastoral poems had survived, they alone would have certainly given Theocritus a claim to being the best of the Alexandrian poets, and certainly the easiest for modern readers to enjoy. It would be doing Theocritus a great injustice, then, not to give his other poems "their proper Laurels."

For purposes of discussion, I have arranged the nonpastoral poems under five headings: mimes *(Idylls X, XIV, XV, II)*, poems on epic themes *(Idylls XXIV, XIII, XXII)*, poems to patrons *(Idylls XVI, XVII)*, paederastic love poems *(Idylls XII, XXIX, XXX)*, and finally miscellaneous poems *(Idylls XVIII, XXVI, XXVIII)* and epigrams. I have not bothered to mention poems which modern scholarship no longer considers to be by Theocritus.

The term "idyll" *(eidullion)* which has traditionally been applied to the longer poems of Theocritus means nothing more than "poem," and should have been discarded long ago, since it is a neutral term and implies nothing "idyllic" about the poems; it is easily confused with the more modern generic term which does indeed suggest peace, tranquillity and life in Arcadian fields. *Idylls I, III - VII,* and *XI* are "pastoral idylls," in the modern sense of the term; the other poems by Theocritus are "poems"—creations of Theocritus' roving inspiration which, like the individual pastoral

85

idylls, lack titles which can be attributed with any certainty to the poet himself.

I *The Four Mimes*

Four major nonpastoral poems of Theocritus (*Idylls X, XIV, XV,* and *II*) may be classified as mimes (see Chapter 4, section II). However, it should be noted that, with the exception of *Idyll VII,* the pastoral idylls are also mimes, whose protagonists happen to be herdsmen-poets rather than the city dwellers we find in the mimes of Theocritus' contemporary, Herondas, and where song and narrative frame are added to the usual structural devices of monologue and dialogue. It is not surprising, then, that the four mimes of Theocritus have much in common with the seven *Pastoral Idylls* thematically as well as formally. The major *difference* is that the element of low mimetic description (of the more vulgar or ordinary side of life) which characterizes the urban mimes of Herondas and Theocritus is subordinated, in the *Pastoral Idylls,* to the presentation of lyrical themes and motifs which make these poems much more than the lively dramatic skits about life in the fields for which they have sometimes been taken.

However, Theocritus' mimes (even *Idyll II,* with its apparently romantic and passionate lyricism) really are nothing more than lively dramatic skits, slice-of-life scenes from the realm of the all-too-human. As such, however, they aim at the maximum poetization of ordinary life possible within the limits of the kind of realism of which they are the most polished Alexandrian examples. The mimes bear witness to Theocritus' fascination with the theme of the impact of love and esthetic beauty on the lives of people living in humble circumstances, a theme which dominates the *Pastoral Idylls,* to the extent that the latter purport to describe the lives of actual herdsmen. But, in the mimes there is none of the irony which informs our sense of the Theocritean herdsman as a synthetic figure who combines the attributes of hired hand and urban literatus. The characters of the four mimes are exactly what they appear to be: field hands, mercenary soldiers, and women—all members of traditionally oppressed social groups whose lives are treated here with a sympathy all too rare in Greek literature.

Idyll X presents a moment of leisure enjoyed by two hard working reapers, who pause for a short dramatic exchange of words and songs. Their days spent in the hot sun contrast with the idle ex-

istence of the herdsmen of the *Pastoral Idylls,* who are always ready
to sing in the shade. The accent put on work is a sign that
Theocritus has left the domain of the pastoral genre with this composition, however ingeniously it transposes pastoral themes and
motifs from the pastures to the cultivated fields.

The first speaker, Milon, is an unsentimental peasant who is
"hard as a rock" (7), and finds it inconceivable that his fellow
reaper Bucaeus should have fallen desperately in love: "what kind
of thing is love for a working man, unless it has to do with his
work?" (9). But Milon, who complains of his sleepless nights in
order to prove his point, insists that he has lost his heart to the Bombyca, the girl who was hired to pipe to the reapers as they worked
(her name, as Gow explains in his note, probably derives from the
name of the type of flute she played, the *bombyx*).[1]

Milon, for all his apparent insensitivity, knows as well as the
Cyclops of *Idyll XI* what may help Bucaeus ease the pain of his
frustrated desire:

> just you keep on reaping
> while you sing a love song for the girl; that way
> you'll take more pleasure in your work—I know you used
> to be a music lover.
> (21 - 23)

Bucaeus' song (24 - 37) is no more than what we would expect
from a figure who parodies, rather than embodies, poetic genius: it
is short and endearingly ridiculous, its main virtue being its sinceri-
ty. In fact, it is similar to the more ambitious composition of the silly goatherd of *Idyll III,* and begins with the same invocation of the
beloved's name (*X* l. 26//*III* l. 6). The reaper's mind, like the
goatherd's and the Cyclops', is full of ridiculously sentimental fan-
tasies. He imagines that if he were as rich as Croesus (the wealth of
Croesus was already proverbial), he would have two gold statues
made as an offering to Aphrodite, one of Bombyca and her pipes,
the other of himself wearing a new pair of shoes! This flight of the
imagination exhausts Bucaeus' poetic inspiration, and his song
stumbles to an embarrassingly grotesque conclusion:

> Lovely Bombyca, your feet are dice players' knucklebones,
> Your voice is a flower, and your ways—are more than I
> can say.
> (36 - 37)

The fact of the matter is that Bombyca is skinny and suntanned (neither characteristic was a mark of female beauty for the Greeks), and Bucaeus is apparently the only one to find her attractive—Milon, for example, calls her a grasshopper (18). The opening of Bucaeus' song, an invocation of the Pierian Muses (cf. opening of *Idyll XI*) is an ironic commentary on his deluded state of mind:

> Pierian Muses, sing with me of the slender girl,
> since whatever you goddesses touch you make beautiful.
> (24 - 25)

Bombyca is beautiful only in his imagination, since her feet are in reality as bony as knucklebone dice; and he really is incapable of describing her "ways" (37), since love prevents him from seeing her as she is.

However, *Idyll X* is not only a humorous commentary on the age-old theme of the lover's blindness to the faults of his beloved. Bombyca may be swarthy and skinny, but she is also a rural musician; her pipes are mentioned in line 16 as well as in line 34, where her golden statue, as imagined by the reaper, holds both pipes and love tokens. Bucaeus is himself a music lover (*mousikos*, l. 23), and it is quite possible that Theocritus is suggesting that Bucaeus is as much in love with her music as with her person—perhaps more so, since it takes the Pierian Muses (24 - 25) to make her beautiful! The themes of love and poetry are joined in this mime with an irony which is highly reminiscent of Theocritus' procedure in the *Pastoral Idylls*. Here also the Theocritean theme of poetry as a cure for love is dominant, at least in the first forty lines of the poem.

What prevents *Idyll X* from moving even more in the direction of pastoral is the figure of Milon, whose compliments to Bucaeus on his song are probably no more than veiled sarcasm (38 - 40). His own songs are all Hesiodic snatches, and represent an attempt on the part of Theocritus to beat the peasant poet of the *Works and Days* at his own game, although he has Milon attribute the snatches to an archetypal composer of work songs, Lityerses. The poem thus ends on a Hesiodic, and not pastoral, note: "These are the songs that men who work in the sun should sing!" (56) In spite of many elements which remind us of the *Pastoral Idylls*, it is the Hesiodic figure of Milon who sets the tone of the mime, not the more bucolic figure of the lovelorn Bucaeus.

Francis Cairns, following the lead of Felix Jacoby, considers both

Idylls X and *XIV* to be examples of a nonrhetorical genre of antiquity (nonrhetorical, that is, "never embraced by rhetoric and . . .
never taught and practiced in the rhetorical schools"),[2] which he
describes as follows: "The addressee, a lover, displays symptoms of
love which arouse speculation or interrogation about the love by the
speaker. The speaker asks or surmises the cause of the symptoms
and/or identity of the beloved, and may comment upon the
beloved." This genre, which had no name in ancient times, Cairns
dubs "symptoms of love."[3] Its origin, he says, is symposiastic, that
is, it originated in *symposia* or drinking parties. Greek men allowed
themselves, as many of us have since, to wax unusually sentimental
and confiding on such occasions: "the symposium is the only context in ancient life in which discussion of this sort normally took
place among good-mannered persons."[4] The mixing of wine and
the wearing of garlands were signs that emotional reserve could be
laid aside. The "symptoms of love" genre ultimately derived from
the kind of drunken conversations which took place at *symposia*,
just as the *paraklausithyron* (cf. the discussion of *Idyll III*) had its
origin in the serenade which followed a symposium, when the lover
wanted more than cautionary advice or sympathy from his friends
and drinking companions, and dragged them with him through the
cold and empty streets toward his beloved's threshold. It is this urban "symptoms of love" genre which Theocritus transposes to the
countryside in *Idyll X*, and which he modifies in *Idyll XIV*,[5] where
the scene most likely takes place on a street corner.

In *Idyll XIV*, two old friends, Aeschinas and Thyonichus, meet
after a long period of absence. Aeschinas displays his "symptoms of
love": an untrimmed mustache, hair grown long and curly, and loss
of weight. He explains that he is pining away for the girl Cynisca,
who left him two months earlier after he had hit her twice with his
fist at a drinking party in the country where she had gotten drunk
and sentimental and had let it be known that she was in love with
someone else. Aeschinas recreates this scene in a monologue of
great low mimetic vigor (12 - 56). But now that two months have
passed, Aeschinas is sick with longing for her, and does not know
what the cure (*pharmakon* 52//*Idyll XI* l. 1) for his love might be.

In the *Pastoral Idylls*, the cure for love was poetry, and even in
Idyll X, which was set in the grain fields, Milon could advise
Bucaeus to sing his amorous blues away. But *Idyll XIV* does not
pick up on this pastoral *topos*. Aeschinas is a simple man with no
talent for esthetic sublimation of the sexual instincts; another

remedy for his love must be found. Fortunately, Aeschinas remembers that another man of his age (his hair is graying, 68 - 70) named Simus, also a victim of a woman's charms, expatriated himself for a while, and came back "cured" (53 - 54). Thyonichus approves of the idea, and suggests that if Aeschinas wants to go abroad for a while, "Ptolemy is the best paymaster for a free man" (59). The mime ends with this clever joining of the Theocritean motif of a cure for love with the praise of Theocritus' patron Ptolemy Philadelphus.

Idyll XV presents a couple of hours in the lives of two Syracusan ladies, Gorgo and Praxinoa, who are living in Alexandria. These female compatriots of Theocritus gossip together for a while (1 - 43), and then step out into the crowded streets of Alexandria, where they make their way, accompanied by their two maidservants, towards the palace precincts of Ptolemy Philadelphus (44 - 77). Queen Arsinoe, sister and wife of Ptolemy after the Egyptian Pharaonic custom, has opened the palace to the public so that the Alexandrian Greeks can view the art works created for this year's Adonis festival, and listen to newly composed hymns in honor of Aphrodite and her young lover, Adonis. One of these hymns (100 - 43) brings the mime to a close, and Gorgo and Praxinoa leave for their homes, delighted with their excursion.

In his essay "Pagan and Mediaeval Religious Sentiment" (1864), Matthew Arnold presented this mime of Theocritus, and more particularly the hymn to Adonis which it contains, as "a representative religious poem of paganism."[6] He was entranced, as I am also, with the liveliness of the dialogue between Gorgo and Praxinoa: "It is a page torn fresh out of the book of human life. What freedom! What animation! What gaiety! What naturalness!"[7] He was not so pleased, however, with the hymn, which "has nothing whatsoever that is elevating, nothing that is consoling, nothing that is in our sense of the word religious."[8] Nevertheless, he did not see the hymn to be the result of any artistic miscalculation on the part of Theocritus; rather, he blamed the pagan religious sense which, in his opinion allowed no scope for anything better. The hymn, the vivacious dialogue of the Syracusan housewives, the cheerful bustle of the streets of Alexandria and the garish pomp of a Ptolemaic festival are all, Arnold implies, equally frivolous: "This Greek hymn adapts itself exactly to the tone and temper of a gay and pleasure-loving multitude."[9]

No doubt, it is hardly fair of Arnold to go on to compare the "religious sentiment" of this hymn to Adonis with the "Canticle of the Sun" of St. Francis of Assisi, one of Christianity's most gifted and colorful mystic-poets. However, it is a good idea, although this was perhaps not Arnold's intention, to ask why Theocritus included a religious hymn in the unlikely context of an urban mime, and whether there is more to *Idyll XV* than can be expressed by Arnold's not altogether undisparaging phrase, "the cheerful sensuous pagan life."

One manifest intention of Theocritus in *Idyll XV* was to celebrate the magnificence of the Ptolemaic court at Alexandria which, thanks to the wealth of the Nile, was able to sponsor such lavish spectacles and processions for the entertainment of the Greek citizenry. Athenaeus has preserved for us a much more detailed description (*Deipnosophistai*, V. 196 - 203) of a procession organized by Ptolemy Philadelphus in honor of the god Dionysos; *Idyll XV* reflects the same taste for pomp and splendor on a smaller scale.

What did Gorgo and Praxinoa actually see? Gow reconstructs the scene in the following manner:

The stage is a room, a marquee, or more probably a garden, inside the Palace precincts, hung with a tapestry representing Adonis in a silver chair, dead or dying,. with Aphrodite and other figures in attendance. In unspecified relation to the tapestry are arbours of greenery, in which are hung bunches of fragrant herbs; above them are suspended flying figures of Erotes. In the central arbour is a couch of ebony and gold, the legs of which are formed of ivory groups of Ganymede carried off by an eagle. On it recline on purple coverlets figures of Adonis and Aphrodite, who embrace or kiss. In front of the couch are tables bearing a lavish display of food. Other arbours are similarly furnished, but the couches are unoccupied and will remain so until the spectators depart and those invited to the feast arrive and take their places on them. The populace who come to view the show are entertained at intervals by singers, who are perhaps taking part in a singing competition. [10]

A number of details in this scene of Alexandrian luxury have religious significance. The festival of Adonis was a manifestation of the tremendous popularity in the ancient world of the cult of the Great Mother and her lover-son. The Great Mother herself was identified with the force which made the fields fertile, and her son was the world's vegetation. Mother and Son formed an archetypal couple of great numinous power, whether known as Ishtar and Tammuz in Babylonia, Isis and Osiris in Egypt, Cybele and Attis in

Asia Minor, or Aphrodite and Adonis among the Greeks. The centerpiece of the display represents the bridal feast of Aphrodite and Adonis, and the divine couple is appropriately offered perfumes and cakes. Adonis, as a vegetation god, is also worshipped with offerings of fruits, bowers of greenery and potted plants (112 - 14, 119 - 20). The whole display might remind a modern Christian of a Christmas *crèche*, which is meant to be viewed and admired for its artfulness as well as for its religious significance.

Aphrodite's love for Adonis had tragic consequences, according to the myth. In the tapestry (78 - 86) Adonis is pictured as dead or dying. The Greek version of the myth had it that Ares, the jealous consort of Aphrodite, sent a wild boar who caused the death of the youth while he was away from Aphrodite on a hunt. Older versions of the story, according to Erich Neumann, have the young vegetation god condemned to death by the Great Mother herself; and in the corresponding rituals, the role of Adonis was taken not by a statue, as here, but by a young man who was offered to the Great Mother as a living sacrifice in order to ensure the fertility of the fields.[11] The archaic religious horror of such a matriarchal religious ritual is no doubt absent from the display centering on the tapestry depicting the dying or dead Adonis, which is more reminiscent of a Christian *Pietà* (where Mary holds the corpse of her dead son Jesus in her lap much after the manner, I would imagine, of the mourning Aphrodite depicted here as well as in *Idyll III* l. 48). In Alexandria the Adonis festival included, as the singer reminds the audience in 132 - 35, a ritualized mourning for Adonis, during which the women would carry the image of the dead god down to the seashore, beat their breasts and make lamentation.

As in the Christian religion, however, the god only dies in order to rise again, just as the vegetation scorched by the late summer sun (the Alexandrian festival took place in August or September) is sure to grow back in the springtime. The hymn to Adonis closes with the joyful anticipation of his annual resurrection:

> Bless us then, Adonis dear,
> And bring us joy another year;
> Dearly hast thou come again,
> And dearly shalt be welcomed then.
>   (ll. 143 - 44, translated by Leigh Hunt)

Gorgo and Praxinoa echo this cheerful farewell to the god in the last line of the mime.

That representations of Adonis and other Middle Eastern dying gods maintain even to this day a power to affect the modern religious temperament, is illustrated by C. G. Jung's reaction to photographs of a Greek marble head of Attis:

The erotic element, the feminine sweetness of the face, the peculiar treatment of the hair on the one hand . . . the juvenile masculinity on the other hand, suggest one of the early dying son-gods of the Near East. I think chiefly of Attis, the son and lover of Kybele. . . . He has, like his *analoga*, viz. Adonis, Tammuz, and the Germanic Baldur, all the grace and charm of either sex. . . . That is about the nearest I can get to a diagnosis of the head and its truly bewitching beauty. At all events it expresses in a perfect way the feeling an Asiatic Greek would experience in worshipping Attis or one of his equivalents, one of the *pueri aeterni*, being the joy of men and women and dying early with the flower of spring.

May I keep at least one of the photos? They have caught my fantasy thoroughly.

A footnote to this letter informs us that "Jung had the photo framed and kept it on his desk."[12]

It is also likely that the myth of the Great Mother and the dying son-god was close to the heart of Theocritus. The evocation of Demeter at the end of *Idyll VII* conveys more of what Matthew Arnold would call "pagan religious sentiment," and the sentiment can only be described as being personal and "Theocritean." The myth of Daphnis, which plays such an important role in the *Pastoral Idylls*, is a particularly tragic variant of the myth, since the Great Mother in the form of Aphrodite is shown both gloating over Daphnis' approaching death and willing but unable to prevent it (cf. *I* ll. 138 - 39). Daphnis is overwhelmed by the forces of Eros, as are the other lovers of the Great Mother mentioned by the goatherd in *Idyll III:* Endymion, Iasion and, again, Adonis (*III* ll. 46 - 51).

Yet for all the grandeur of the myth, and Theocritus' interest in its deeper resonances, the hymn to Aphrodite and Adonis is a deliberately parodistic example of Alexandrian kitsch. K. J. Dover, who shares Arnold's disappointment with the piece, writes in his recent commentary: "I should have expected Theokritos to take the opportunity of showing how well he could write a hymn, not the opportunity of showing how badly most people wrote them; but this expectation founders on the hymn we have before us." He points to "the hyperbolic effusion of 123" and "the clumsy rampage through mythology in 137ff." and suggests that Theocritus wrote "a sly parody of the songs characteristic of these occasions and applauded by audiences whose thoughts and tastes, like those of Gorgo and Praxinoa, existed only as strings of clichés."[13]

The whole second part of *Idyll XV* is thus a mixture of the sublime and the ridiculous. There is the sublimity of the theme, a resurrection myth which, Matthew Arnold conceded, "symbolically treated, . . . as the Greek mysteries undoubtedly treated it, . . . could lead the soul to elevating and consoling thoughts."[14] Then there is what we might term the politicization of that theme, a hymn which is designed to impress on the crowd the glory and generosity of Queen Arsinoe as much as the religious dimensions of the myth. Theocritus' realism is thus a critical realism: through a sophisticatedly ironic presentation of his material, he provides us with a lively commentary on the state of Alexandrian popular culture manipulated by the Ptolemaic artistic establishment.

But Theocritus' irony is gentle, not savage. His presentation of Gorgo and Praxinoa in *Idyll XV* is analogous to his presentation of the herdsmen of the *Pastoral Idylls*. In both cases he is fascinated with the theme of the power of art to affect alert but unsophisticated minds. It is this theme, rather than "religious sentiment," which Theocritus is interested in communicating in *Idyll XV*. His portrayal of Gorgo and Praxinoa is sympathetic, and although he does not conceal the vulgarity of their artistic tastes, he makes the hymn to Adonis as much of a genuine esthetic experience for them as the pastoral songs, with their similar mixture of the ridiculous and the sublime, were for the herdsmen-poets of the *Pastoral Idylls*. By presenting this theme of the power of art to affect unsophisticated minds in the urban context of the Alexandria of his day, Theocritus extended the range of what was for him no doubt originally a pastoral theme.

The description of a day in the lives of two Syracusan ladies marks another extension of the art of Theocritus. Greek literature rarely attempted to portray the day-to-day life of women, the things they did and said when no man was present or listening. *Idyll XV* is an especially interesting combination of poetry and realism, and treats the daily life of women with unusual sympathy and sensitivity. Theocritus deliberately joins an ironic presentation of a hymn associated with the mysteries of the originally matriarchal cult of the Great Mother with a low mimetic description of two women living out the feminine condition as experienced by middle-class ladies of the *oikoumenē*.

The conversation between Gorgo and Praxinoa reveals that Praxinoa believes that her husband Dinon moved the family far away
from Gorgo's house in order to break up the friendship of the two
women (7 - 10), and that this is his usual attitude towards female
friendship. Nevertheless, the two are determined to continue their
friendship in spite of Dinon's male chauvinist objections to female
bonding; their excursion to the *Adonia* at the Palace precincts is
thus both a manifestation of their interest in a religious cult
traditionally associated with women and the Great Mother of the
matriarchal period, and a sign of their will to maintain their
friendship. The aggressive tone which they are able to take toward
men is seen not only in what they say about their husbands' inabili-
ty to do shopping intelligently (15 - 17, 18 - 20), but also in an exchange with a man who makes the mistake of ridiculing their
Dorian accents and gets a spirited tongue-lashing in return (87 -
95).

Idyll II is the culmination of Theocritus' efforts to portray the
feminine condition in the *oikoumenē*. The heroine of this mime,
Simaetha, like her male counterpart Aeschinas in *Idyll XIV*, has
been jilted by her lover. She, however, is not about to reconcile
herself to the pain of separation, and the first part of her nocturnal
monologue consists primarily of a series of magic incantations and
prayers to the feminine divinities of the night, magic, and love
(Selene, goddess of the Moon; Hecate; Aphrodite; and Artemis)
designed to make her lover return (1 - 63). This part of the poem is
governed by the refrain "Iynx, bring that man back to my house."
The "iynx" was a magic wheel which, as Detienne has shown, had
strong symbolic associations with extramarital love.[15] Simaetha is
not after a husband, but is rather in the grip of a blind passion for a
handsome youth, Delphis. She tells the story of her infatuation with
Delphis in the second part of her monologue (64 - 158), which is
governed by the appropriate refrain "Show how my love began, O
goddess of the Moon." The last lines of the poem (159 - 166) return
to the theme of magic, but *Idyll II* ends on an unexpected note of
serenity with Simaetha's farewell to the Moon.

The mime is unusually colorful and atmospheric in its evocation
of magic rites in the lonely hours of the night. It is also an unusually
realistic portrayal of a woman in a state of passionate obsession.
Although Greek mythology was full of tales of the passionate encounters of nymphs and goddesses with mortal men, sexual passion
was a state of mind which Greek literature before Theocritus did

not care much to examine in women; Euripides' Phaedra was the most obvious exception.

Simaetha's description of her uncomplicated physical passion for Delphis leaves open the question of why Greek literature, which was largely created for and by men, could portray goddesses, but avoided description of the passionate woman with sex on her mind. Erich Neumann offers one explanation for the fact; although it can hardly be said to apply to all times and places, it probably fits the Greek world well enough, which by the time of Theocritus was at least beginning to overcome some of its patriarchal fear of women and was becoming more willing to see women on equal terms with men:

The emotional, passionate nature of the female in wild abandon is a terrible thing for man and his consciousness. The dangerous side of woman's lasciviousness, although suppressed, misunderstood, and minimized in patriarchal times, was still a living experience in earlier ages. Deep down in the evolutionary stratum of adolescence, the fear of it still dwells in every man and works like a poison wherever a false conscious attitude represses this layer of reality into the unconscious.[16]

This passage follows Neumann's description of the human sacrifice offered up to the Great Mother; Simaetha, of course, wishes mainly to regain Delphis as a lover, but she ends her magic by threatening to poison him (159 - 62), if things do not turn out as she desires. Simaetha, during the period she spends communing with Hecate, is living in the world of matriarchal power, where spells can magically bind a lover, and drugs can cause his death if he continues to be unfaithful.

The account which Simaetha gives of her love affair with Delphis (64 - 158) is remarkably straightforward. She has sent away her female slave to spread her magic concoctions on Delphis' threshold, and now that she is alone with the moon overhead, she can be completely candid. She first saw Delphis, she says, when she was returning from a festival to Artemis (64 - 80), and right away she desired the young man who was freshly oiled down after a workout in the *gymnasion* or wrestling school: "I saw him, I went mad, and my poor heart caught fire" (82 - 83). Her "symptoms of love" are described in the following stanza (88 - 92), and by the next she is telling her slave to go to the wrestling school and give Delphis a message which can only be described as being very much to the point: "Simaetha asks you to come" (101). Delphis arrives posthaste; he is, it would seem, somewhat surprised if not disconcerted by the directness of her proposal, since he rambles on for a while about how eager he would have been to serenade her, content himself with a kiss, or break down her door with the violence born of true passion (118 - 28)—this traditional *kōmos* being absolutely unnecessary under the circumstances, since it is Simaetha who has played the active role in this scene where the usual sexual roles of male lover and female (or boy) beloved have been reversed. It is appropriate, and rather comic at the same time, that the only reply which Simaetha makes to the rather vapid amorous conceits which the young man no doubt feels are required by the occasion (130 - 38), is to take him by the hand and pull him down onto the bed (138 - 39).

Although Simaetha's passion for Delphis seems quite uncomplicated by questions of pregnancy, romantic love, marriage, or money, it has nevertheless been subject to a certain amount of misinterpretation. Alfred Koerte, for example, had this to say:

In this poem, as it seems to me, an age-old yet perennially new poetic motif is developed in a straightforward manner, without erudite flourishes or overrefinement of style. The maid who surrenders herself freely to her beloved, strong in the faith that their mutual love will abide forever, and then must needs experience man's fickleness, has been a subject for innumerable poets; but seldom has she been portrayed more simply and impressively than by Theocritus. [17]

However, it is simply not true that Simaetha plays Gretchen to Delphis' Faust. Even Charles Segal falls into the trap of presenting Delphis as "the archetypal seducer" who leaves Simaetha in a hopeless situation.[18] One forgets too easily that it was Simaetha who seduced Delphis, and that she is willing to try anything, including murder, to see to it that she will not have to play the role of the helpless forsaken maiden which the male imagination might prefer to foist upon her.

Gow's note on the "love-at-first-sight during or after a festival" in line 66 is more pertinent: "Theocritus has enlivened this hackneyed theme with a striking variant, for it is usually the man, not the woman, who falls a victim to such love at first sight." In fact, sexual roles are reversed throughout *Idyll II*, which may be termed a "striking variant" on the more general theme of seduction. It is

Simaetha, a woman, who falls in love at first sight, makes the first moves (94 - 103), plays the role in seduction which was normally delegated to the man (thus leaving Delphis unable to get together the usual *kōmos* in her honor), and employs a bit of physical force in order to hasten the consummation of their union (138 - 39). After Delphis' unexplained absence and presumed infidelity, Simaetha is also given the traditionally male role of the forlorn lover to play (cf. Aratus in *Idyll VII*, who also has a rival to confront), and her maid's journey to spread the magic concoction on Delphis' threshold (59 - 62) corresponds roughly to the journey to the closed or bolted door which the male *kōmastēs* would undertake as a necessary part of his wooing.

If Simaetha's magic incantations do not bring her back her lover by the end of the mime, they have at least put her in contact with the feminine powers of darkness, the surviving matriarchal forces of feminine strength and endurance. By the end of her monologue Simaetha has been utterly candid (the moon's light has, as it were, shown her her situation with the greatest possible clarity); she also seems to have attained some of the serenity of the moon and the starlit sky, although there may be some irony in the final lines:

> I will go on bearing the burden of my longing now as before.
> Farewell, Selene of the gleaming throne, and farewell, you
>   other
> stars, followers of serene Night's chariot.
>   (164 - 66)

In the contemplation of the heavens, an activity which took on new meaning in Hellenistic times thanks to the new schools of philosophy, Simaetha finds some of the *hasychia* or mental peace which Aratus or Lycidas in *Idyll VII* seek as a cure fo the violence of their passions. The portrayal which Theocritus has given of her desperate desire for Delphis puts her in the same category as the other passionate lovers of the *Idylls*, who are cruelly afflicted by Eros and driven to seek satisfaction where satisfaction cannot be found. That Simaetha is a woman is the only unusual factor; as a woman, she is presented not as the "Other," but as an equal partner of the male protagonists in the *Idylls* who are involved in the search for erotic fulfillment and a cure for their painful obsessions.

II   *Poems on Epic Themes*

Three poems of Theocritus narrate scenes from the lives of legendary heroes from a peculiarly Alexandrian perspective. It has been customary to label these poems on epic themes *epyllia* (sing. *epyllion*) or "little epics," but, as Dover has pointed out, the term is a late one in antiquity and probably did not designate such poems as *Idylls XXIV, XIII,* and *XXII.*[19] These three poems illustrate an Alexandrian approach to the epic genre which abandoned the attempt to rival the Homeric tradition; an approach which employed humor as well as reverence, and was later to be mastered by the Roman poets (Propertius *Book IV* and Ovid's *Fasti*).

Two of Theocritus' poems on epic themes (*Idylls XXIV* and *XIII*) narrate scenes from the life of the Greek hero, Heracles. Heracles was the son of Zeus and Alcmena, a mortal woman. After accomplishing his twelve heroic labors, Heracles became immortal and went to dwell with his divine father on Olympus (cf. *Idyll XXIV* ll. 79 - 83). Ptolemy Philadelphus traced his descent from Heracles (cf. *Idyll XVII* ll. 13 - 33), and it is possible that his patron's pride in his heroic ancestry was the original stimulus for Theocritus' two poems as well as for two others in the same vein, the so-called *Herakles Leontofonos* ("Heracles the Lion Killer," *Idyll XXV*) and the *Megara* (Moschus *IV*), which have been incorrectly attributed to Theocritus.

Idyll XXIV, the *Herakliskos* or "Little Heracles," deals with the folkloric motif of the newborn prodigy. In a rather charming piece of Hellenistic epic narration, Theocritus tells the story of how the ten-month-old Heracles strangled the serpents which Hera, ever jealous over Zeus' philandering with mortal women, sent to destroy Alcmena's semidivine child as he lay sleeping in the brazen shield which served as his cradle (1 - 63). After the heroic deed is done and the excitement is over, Alcmena calls for the seer Teiresias, who prophecies Heracles' future labors and immortality (64 - 102). Theocritus goes on to describe the education of the young hero in lines 103 to 140, at which point the text breaks off. A nearly illegible papyrus fragment of the remaining thirty lines or so seems to indicate that the poem ended with Theocritus' prayer for Heracles' assistance in winning a poetic competition. One easily arrives at the hypothesis that the poem was created for an Alexandrian poetic competition in honor of the divine ancestor of the Ptolemaic dynasty. This would explain the contrast between the fine Theocritean workmanship and the un-Theocritean nature of the theme in a poem which seems more commissioned than inspired.

As Gow has noted, Theocritus "follows the narration of Pindar in his first Nemean ode but he is at pains to reduce it from an heroic to a domestic level."[20] This "domestication" of epic themes was a general tendency of Hellenistic writers who wrote in the wake of Callimachus' *Hecalē*. It is unusual for Theocritus to pattern his narrative so exactly after another model (see Dover's introduction to the poem for the parallels); but this may be another sign that this "piece of Hellenistic Biedermeier,"[21] as Galinsky calls it, was a commissioned work.

Idyll XIII ("Hylas") provides the best instance of how Theocritus' genius could grapple successfully with the problems of creating epic narrative in an age of "the obsolescence of epic."[22] In *Idyll XIII* Heracles is desperately in love with the boy Hylas; the heroic side of his character is completely overshadowed by his Hellenistic—and Theocritean—vulnerability to Eros. Heracles has taken his beloved with him on board the Argo (5 - 24), the ship which was carrying Jason and the Argonauts on their quest of the Golden Fleece. The heroes land one evening on the shores of the Propontis (between the Hellespont and the Black Sea), and Hylas is sent to fetch water for Heracles and his messmate Telamon (25 - 39). Wandering around in the twilight, Hylas comes upon a spring where, unknown to him, nymphs are dancing in the dark water. Hylas bends down to dip his pitcher, only to be pulled into the water by the nymphs, who have developed a sudden passion for the beautiful boy. As the nymphs console Hylas for his quick departure frm the world of mortal men (he is now one of the blessed immortals, cf. 72), Heracles searches desperately for his beloved; he shouts his name three times near the spring, "but faint came Hylas' answering cry from the water, and far off he seemed though very near at hand" (ll. 59 - 60, Gow's translation).

Tennyson was extremely moved by the beauty of this idyll, according to Palgrave:

We were sitting (1857 or so) late at night in the Farringford attic-room . . . and Tennyson read over to me the little Theocritean Idyll *Hylas*, eminent for beauty in a treasure-house where all are beautiful. He dwelt particularly on the tender loveliness of the lines which describe how the fair youth, carried to the depths of a fountain by the enamored Nymphs, faintly answered the call of his companion Herakles. . . . "I should be content to die," said the author of the "English Idyls," and of the "Idylls of the King," "if I had written anything equal to this."[23]

Idyll XIII succeeds as a poem on an epic theme because it is closest to that pastoral inspiration which Theocritus could ill afford to exchange for less congenial Muses. The desperate passion of Heracles, itself a pastoral theme in the context of the Theocritean corpus, is given an appropriately pastoral setting. The descriptions of the meadows where the Argonauts take their evening rest before sailing at midnight (33 - 35) and of the spring and its dancing nymphs (39 - 45), are fine Theocritean pastoral touches, and the nocturnal atmosphere of mystery and magic is reminiscent of *Idyll II*. The simile which follows the description of Hylas' sudden abduction by the water nymphs is especially noteworthy; Leigh Hunt's translation catches some of the sweet mysteriousness of the passage which must have appealed to Tennyson:

> Down stepped the boy, in haste to give his urn
> Its fill, and pushed it in the fount; when lo!
> Fair hands were on him—fair, and very fast;
> For all the gentle souls that haunted there
> Were drawn in love's sweet yearning tow'rds the boy;
> And so he dropped within the darksome well—
> Dropped like a star, that, on a summer eve,
> Slides in ethereal beauty to the sea.
> (ll. 46 - 52)

But Leigh Hunt was clearly baffled by the last line and a half of the simile, which he chose not to translate:

> . . . as when a shooting star falls
> suddenly into the sea, *and some sailor says to his mates:*
> *"Make ready, boys, the wind is right for sailing."*
> (my italics)

A shooting star was a sign of rising winds for Greek sailors; the association of Hylas' fall with a shooting star, which is in turn associated with sailors setting out to sea, is a fine example of anticipatory irony, since the Argonauts are soon to set sail and leave Hylas and the frantic Heracles behind. Recent commentators have appreciated this sudden twist of Theocritus' epic simile more than Leigh Hunt and earlier commentators. Donald, Mastronarde notes that "the poet shifts back to reality with the sailor's startlingly practical utterance";[24] and Charles Segal observes that the second part of the simile "evokes the situation in the mortal world from which Hylas is cut off"; it "jarringly conjoins the heroic and the fairytale narratives."[25]

Idyll XIII opens with some words addressed to Nicias, the amorous doctor or medical student of the frame of *Idyll XI:*

> Eros was not brought into this world just for our sake,
>   as we once believed,
> Nicias, by whichever one of the gods engendered him;
> nor are we the first to see beauty as beautiful,
> (mortals that we are, who know not what tomorrow brings):
> even the mighty son of Amphitryon, ironhearted,
> he who braved the savage lion, was in love with a boy,
> the lovely Hylas. . . .
>   (1 - 7)

The implied comparison between the legendary hero and the two friends (reminiscing, as it seems, about their student years on Cos and their first discovery of the world of Eros and the pain of love) brings the great Heracles down to the level of everyday life and love in the *oikoumenē*—after all, Heracles also lost his heart to a boy! Thus the whole epic scene can be read as an erotic *paraenesis* addressed to Nicias; the implied advice, according to T. B. L. Webster's comments on the last lines which describe how Heracles rejoined the Argonauts some time after Hylas' death and was mocked as a deserter (72 - 75), is "that however much he indulges in love-affairs he will have to return to his ordinary life as a doctor in the end."[26] Theocritus was right: Nicias got married and settled down as a doctor in his native Miletus (cf. *Idyll XXVIII*).

Idyll XXII ("the Dioscuri") takes the form of a hymn to the divine twins Castor and Polydeuces (Lat. Pollux). It is a diptych, and its first half (27 - 134) describes how Polydeuces won a boxing match with the insolent Amycus. Leigh Hunt wrote an amusing paraphrase and summary of this section of the poem (in *A Jar of Honey from Mount Hybla*, 1848), in which he gives a running commentary on this ancient "Prizefight"—certainly the poem had, and would have now, the greatest attraction for sports fans. As in *Idyll XIII*, the main scene takes place by a spring, described in typically

Theocritean pastoral terms (37 - 43). The fight between Polydeuces and Amycus was also part of the epic cycle of the Argonauts. Apollonius of Rhodes treated this scene in Book *II* (ll. 1 - 97) of the *Argonautica,* and critics have exhausted themselves in the attempt to demonstrate which is the earlier or the better piece of verse (see Chapter 4, section III).

The second part of *Idyll XXII* (ll. 137 - 211) describes a duel between Castor and Lynceus; it is one of the low points in Theocritus' poetic career. "It is largely a pastiche from the *Iliad,*" says Gow, "which can have cost Theocritus, familiar as he was with Homer, but little pains."[27] The Dioscuri were the object of a cult in Alexandria. Ptolemy Philadelphus and his sister Arsinoe were, at least for the Egyptian population, divine siblings in the tradition of the Pharaohs, and Ptolemy's dead parents, Ptolemy Soter and Berenike, were worshipped as a divine couple. Perhaps this hymn on the Divine Twins of Greek mythology was in its final and rather unsatisfactory form the result of a Ptolemaic commission for some official occasion.

III   *Poems to Patrons*

"I am looking for the man who will welcome me and the Muses," says Theocritus in *Idyll XVI* ll. 68 - 69. Without patronage a poet's life was a hard one, and Theocritus knew that kings and tyrants were the best patrons of the age. Two of his poems are addressed to royal patrons, *Idyll XVI* ("The Graces") to Hiero II of Syracuse, and *Idyll XVII* ("The Encomium of Ptolemy") to Ptolemy II Philadelphus of Egypt.

Establishing a proper relationship with one's patron was traditionally a tricky business for the aspiring poet. A tyrant newly established in his dictatorial powers, even when he was *philomousos* (*XIV* l. 61) and a true devotee of the arts, was frequently a violent and insecure human being to deal with; and the closer one came to him, the greater was the danger. Theocritus, having been raised in Syracuse, probably knew that Dionysius of Syracuse had sent the poet Philoxenus to the quarries for involving himself too intimately with the tyrant's mistress Galatea (see Chapter 1, section I). Theocritus' own patron Ptolemy, if the story recorded by Athenaeus is correct (Ath. 14.621A), imprisoned the poet Sotades for criticizing his marriage to his sister Arsinoe, and later had him locked in a chest and drowned. J. M. Edmonds has argued that Theocritus' ver-

sion of the myth of Comatas locked up in a chest "through the im-
pious brutality of a king" (*VII* l. 78 - 79) had something to do with
the Sotades affair.[28] If so, Theocritus' actual attitude towards tyranny, however sweetened by the generous patronage of Ptolemy
Philadelphus, was perhaps more critical than might have been expected from a Sicilian Greek conditioned by a series of tyrannical
regimes in his own native city. A scholiast on Ovid's *Ibis* I l. 549 has
preserved an account of Theocritus' final hours, which most scholars
have ignored, but which Edmonds accredited and translated as
follows:

The Syracusan poet Theocritus . . . was arrested by king Hiero for making
an attack upon his son, the king's object being merely to make him think
that he was going to be put to death. But when Hiero asked him if he
would avoid abusing his son in future, he began to abuse him all the more,
and not only the son but the father too. Whereat the king in indignation
ordered him to be put to death in real earnest, and according to some
authorities he was strangled and according to others beheaded.[29]

This king Hiero would have been the same ruler whose patronage
Theocritus had once solicited, apparently with no success, probably
at the beginning of his career as a poet and Hiero's career as a
tyrant.

   Idyll XVI ("The Graces") is the record of Theocritus' early
dealings with Hiero II of Syracuse. It is one of his better poems.
Landor wrote of it in 1842 that "the best of Pindar's odes is not
more energetic throughout";[30] and Gow added that "the two main
themes—the importance of employing poets (22 - 57) and the
prayer for Syracuse (71 - 100)—are handled in passages of sustained
beauty not surpassed elsewhere by Theocritus."[31]

   However, the poem is rather bizarre, considered strictly as a plea
for patronage. Hiero II was, like Theocritus, a man of common
origin; after his rise to power, he took the name of Hiero, the
famous fifth-century ruler of Syracuse, for whose patronage the
great Pindar rivalled with Bacchylides. *Idyll XVI* echoes with Pin-
daric reminiscences, but it is surprising that no direct mention is
made of the most illustrious of Theocritus' predecessors to seek
favor at the court of Syracuse. Rather, it is Simonides (the "divine
singer of Ceos" of line 44) whose example is cited to prove that
poets have the power to immortalize the names of their patrons
(36 - 47). But Theocritus' choice of Simonides as his *exemplum* is
doubly troublesome. As Norman Austin has pointed out, Simonides

had the reputation of being the archetypal mercenary poet in antiquity, and "we should expect that if Theocritus wished to write a poem asking for patronage, in which the topic of money was to figure so prominently, he would have taken pains to dissociate himself from any possible connection with Simonides."[32]

Another problem arises from the fact that Hiero's name is not even mentioned until the poem is almost three-quarters of the way through (80) and Theocritus has finished berating men of wealth and power who fail to give poets their due, in two passages which demonstrate an unexpected talent for bitter satire (14 - 23, 60 - 65). Nor is Hiero expressly excluded from their company. It is a strange thing indeed for Theocritus to bid for patronage by suggesting that his future patron Hiero II may be no more generous than the stupid skinflints who are ridiculed in the earlier passages of the poem, especially when the example of Hiero I, a generous patron of the arts, was there for the taking.

It is impossible not to ask whether *Idyll XVI* might be less a bid for patronage than a bitter commentary on the poet's failure to find patronage, even in his own native land. If so, it is understandable that Theocritus refrained from criticizing Hiero directly, since this would have closed all doors to future patronage and increased the chances of a permanent exile from Syracuse. After all, Hiero was just consolidating his power at the probable date of composition of *Idyll XVI*, and had perhaps as yet little time or energy for welcoming Theocritus' *charites* or "Graces," that is, his personified manuscripts, which Theocritus must return to their home in the bottom of their box (9 - 11).

As a poem of exile or anticipation of exile, a complaint rather than a plea, it is appropriate that *Idyll XVI* contains a heartfelt prayer to Zeus, Athena, and Persephone to save Theocritus' threatened homeland from the onslaughts of the Carthaginians. The following benediction is especially moving, with its suggestion of swords beaten into ploughshares and its mixing of pastoral and heroic motifs:

> Let Sicilians once again till their fertile fields, and
>   countless
> thousands of sheep fatten in the pastures and bleat o'er
>   the plains,
> and herds of cattle returning home at twilight
> make the traveller hasten onwards to his destination.

> Let the fallow ground be prepared for seeding, while high
>   in the leaves
> the cicada looks down on the shepherds in the sun, and
>   sings.
> Let spiders spin their gossamer webs over weapons and
>   armor,
> and the word "battle cry" perish from our vocabulary.
>   (ll. 90 - 97)

"If no one calls me, I'll stay put—but to the one who calls me, I will go with my Muses and a cheerful heart" (*XVI* ll. 106 - 107). It seems that Theocritus did not have to stay put after all, since Ptolemy Philadelphus eventually called him and his Muses to Alexandria. *Idyll XVII* ("The Encomium of Ptolemy") was no doubt accepted as a proper return for Ptolemy's investment in Theocritus, and the modern reader is likely to see in it no more than that. It lacks the ambiguity and personal feeling which make *Idyll XVI* such a fascinating poem. Theocritus owed *Idyll XVI* to himself—almost as a consolation, I would say; but *Idyll XVII* was something that he owed to Ptolemy. The poem indicates that Theocritus knew how to express gratitude when such an expression was due. *Idyll XVII* has understandably received little favorable comment from scholars and critics, although Francis Cairns has recently made a case for a more favorable evaluation of the poem as "a dignified *basilikos logos*, suited to its addressee and yet free from servile adulation."[33]

IV   *Paederastic Love Poems*

Three of Theocritus' poems (*Idylls XII, XXIX,* and *XXX*) deal with the theme of paederastic love. They are more personal in tone than most of the poet's work, but they hardly constitute a subjective confession of any sort, nor do they anticipate the great achievements of the Roman subjective-erotic elegy. They are, in the main, Theocritean variations on a Greek theme which in its day was as hackneyed and as stereotyped as the modern Hollywood love story.

Greek paederasty, according to George Devereux, was "a kind of luxury product, perpetuated by being assigned an overinflated value. Greek homosexual courtship was 'conspicuous display' in Veblen's sense. It was highly stylized; it was ostentatious and elaborately chivalrous."[34] It was thus in one sense analogous to the later European cultural fashion of courtly love—that is, it was more a matter of public posture than of private sexual orientation; it was an elaborate game whose rewards were more social than sexual. Of course, there was no Kinsey to record the actual sexual habits of the Greeks, and paederasty as well as every other form of Greek sexual expression is known to us primarily through its depiction in literature, although the evidence of the visual arts is not to be slighted. To be an unsuccessful lover of a boy (a common situation, since Greek boys were encouraged not to be free with their sexual favors) was no disgrace; on the contrary, it made the unhappy lover into the center of attention for his sympathetic friends, and provided the occasion for endless conversations at *symposia*, as well as for an occasional *kōmos* afterwards.

Yet Greek paederasty was surely not only a matter of "conspicuous display." One can take Matthew Arnold's notion of "the cheerful sensuous pagan life" with a grain of salt, and still admit that, in comparison with modern industrial civilization, Greek culture was more openly hedonistic, and that it was as leisure loving as it was pleasure loving, thanks to the system of slavery which exempted many free males from the ancient equivalent of the forty-hour week. Yet Greek culture also seems, again in comparison with modern civilization, to have suffered from the historical misfortune of flourishing at a particular point in time when thé patriarchal family was newly established and was prone to all the violent repressiveness of a social system whose authority was as yet not universally respected. Even for a free male, the penalties for adultery or seduction of an unmarried girl could be severe, and tended to put both younger and older women out of the reach of all except the most daring, or foolhardy, lovers. For *l'homme moyen sensuel* who desired something more than the predictable pleasures of venial love (both heterosexual and homosexual), to gain the love of a boy was a realistic ambition. No doubt, young women like Simaetha (*Idyll II*) also existed who supported themselves through some sort of gainful employment, and could, like her, choose their lovers; but literature provides us with little information about them. In all events, as Dover has observed, "the average Greek . . . could be attracted indifferently to a pretty girl or a handsome youth."[35] From the standpoint of the social risk involved, however, one was less likely to create complications by choosing the handsome youth.

However, an affair with a boy had more than negative advantages for the adult Greek male. No doubt, it was a low-risk situation which gave him something to do with his leisure, of which he en-

joyed a good deal more than his modern equivalent, if he were at all
well off; but it also involved him in a pedagogic relationship which
was emotionally and intellectually stimulating, and which would
not have come off as well with a girl in a society where the sexes
were segregated at an early age and had no shared educational experiences.[36] George Devereux refers to the phenomenon of
"displaced fathering" (cf. Heracles' paternal relationship to Hylas
in *Idyll XIII* ll. 8 - 9), which must have contributed a strong
emotional tone to paederastic relationships: "The Greek father
usually failed to counsel his son; instead, he counseled another
man's son, in whom he was erotically interested. As for the boy,
who needed an effective father to model himself upon, he had to
rely upon his *erastēs*, who also served as a father surrogate."[37]
Devereux also saw the culture of classical Greece as presenting some
of the characteristics of a "youth culture";[38] paederastic affairs thus
enabled the Greek male to maintain contact with the much admired
world of adolescence as well as to continue adolescent homosexual
play into his adult years.

One final point needs emphasis, given the differing attitudes
toward homosexual love in the modern world and the corresponding
likelihood of misinterpreting Greek paederasty: Greek paederasty
was traditionally viewed as part of the process of growth toward
adult heterosexuality in marriage. The boy or adolescent was first
courted as a beloved *(erōmenos)*; after his beard had grown, he
courted boys in turn, and went through all the activities and "symptoms of love" associated with the role of the active lover *(erastēs)*.
At last, having sown his wild oats after the Greek fashion, he settled
into marriage. But even then, if Devereux is correct in this matter,
his paederastic years were not necessarily over, since he was likely
to neglect his own son in favor of someone else's son, toward whom
he maintained an erotic interest, and with whom he engaged in
"displaced fathering," if nothing else.

Such, at least, are the theoretical outlines of what might have
happened over much of Greek history in the private world of sex.
The *éducation sentimentale* of the well-off young man of antiquity
also included, of course, ample opportunities for heterosexual contact with *hetaerae* or courtesans, since it was primarily designed to
leave the patriarchal family untroubled and uncontested. There
were, ideally, no virgins seduced, no adultery, no alien offspring, no
cuckoldry—in short, none of the stock devices of the sexual comedy
of Theocritus' age as well as of later centuries of Western civiliza-

tion. At the same time, it allowed considerable freedom for sexual experimentation and for the experiencing of the joys and sorrows of free love.

Having said this much on the frequently misunderstood topic of Greek paederasty, little remains to be said about Theocritus' poems on such a stereotyped subject, since they are among his least original productions. In addition, they provide us with little information about Theocritus' life and loves; we have no idea whether Theocritus married or not, whether he had children or not, whether he really loved "Myrto" (a girl's name mentioned in connection with Theocritus-Simichidas' happy passion in *Idyll VII* ll. 96 - 97) more than goats love springtime, or whether he led a life of Epicurean restraint, a few infatuations now and then interrupting his *hasychia*. A Roman elegist would have given us more glimpses into the troubled world of the passionate soul; a Greek poet was less likely to consider his private life a matter for public discussion.

Idyll XII is, says Webster, a "pretty poem";[39] Gow is not impressed with it.[40] But both Giangrande and Cairns have found it worthy of attention, at least from the standpoint of generic analysis. For Giangrande *Idyll XII* is a humorous specimen of the Hellenistic genre of the *epibaterion*, in which the speaker expresses joy over the return of a beloved (cf. the opening, "You have come, dear boy, after two days and nights," etc.).[41] In *Idyll XII* the speaker is usually assumed to be the poet himself, but Giangrande insists that the speaker is actually a country yokel who apes Alexandrian sophistication,[42] with the humorous results of the sort which we have found in the silly goatherd's *paraklausithyron* in *Idyll III*. Cairns prefers the generic term *prosphoneticon*, and analyzes *Idyll XII* at length from the standpoint of its "sophisticated use of generic topoi."[43] Cairns concludes that *Idyll XII* is "a typical piece of Alexandrian poetry, combining emotional sophistication, generic sophistication, and glossological and aetiological learning"[44] (for the last point, the origin of kissing contests among boys, see *XII* ll. 27 - 34).

In *Idyll XXIX* the poet, who seems to enjoy pulling rank as the *erastēs*, advises a flighty boy not to be fickle: "build one nest only on a single tree" (12). This quasi-paternal exhortation, with its echoes of paederastic *paideia* and displaced fathering, is reinforced with what one imagines were the usual arguments in favor of sexual fidelity: that the boy's reputation is at stake (21 - 22; the paederastic double standard encouraged the *erastēs* to "score," but

shamed the *erōmenos* if he yielded);[45] that he too will grow old one
day (25 - 29) and should act more responsibly; that an old friend
should not be treated the same way as a recent acquaintance (16 -
18); and, as a clincher, that the poet will break up with him immediately if the boy does not pay proper attention to his lover's
words (35 - 40). *Idyll XII* can be read as an illustration of how hard
it was in antiquity to maintain one's position as an *erastēs*, since the
typical adolescent *erōmenos* was undergoing a period of rapid
change and growth, with the usual revolt against paternal or
"displaced" paternal authority. In addition, the *erastēs* was considered to enjoy the lion's share of the physical pleasure of a
paederastic relationship, and the *erōmenos* was thus considered unlikely to return his lover's affection with equal intensity.[46]

Idyll XXX, for all its stereotyped imagery, is the most
"Theocritean" of the three poems on the theme of paederastic love.
As in *Idyll XI*, passion is presented as a kind of disease (1), and the
poet tries to reason with his affective self (*thymos*, 11) in order to
cure himself with good advice. He tells himself that he is too old to
love boys (13 - 17), and he ends his self-admonition with the following gloomy picture of the aging *erastēs* of an adolescent *erōmenos:*

> For the beloved, life races on like a deer in flight,
> and he is always ready to sail in a new direction;
> and his sweet youth blossoms among those of his own age.
> But the lover, to the very marrow of his bones, is consumed
>   by desire.
> Memories obsess his mind; many are the dreams that
>   plague him at night,
> and a year's time is too short to bring his dread
>   disease to an end.
>   (18 - 23)

But such Theocritean and Epicurean reasoning is no match for the
wisdom of the heart. Eros, who rules over Zeus and even over Venus
herself, is hardly to be mastered by a mortal man (25 - 32), and
Theocritus admits that he must yield to his heart (*thymos*), and go
on loving the boy.

V *Miscellaneous Poems and Epigrams*

Of the remaining poems of Theocritus, *Idyll XXVIII* ("The
Distaff") and *Epigram 8* were inspired by the long-term friendship

between the poet and Nicias. Theocritus apparently sailed to Miletus (*XXVIII* ll. 5 - 7) some time after his doctor friend's marriage, and brought Nicias' wife Theugenis an ivory distaff of Syracusan workmanship; *Idyll XXVIII* was no doubt written to accompany the gift. It is a poem full of warm feeling for both Nicias and his wife. In its own delicate way, it is a monument to Epicurean friendship. *Epigram 8* also dates from the period of Nicias' establishment as a doctor in his native Miletus; it commemorates a cedarwood statue of Asclepius which Nicias had commissioned and set up for his personal worship of the god of healing.

Idylls *XVIII* ("Helen's Epithalamium") and *XXVI* ("The Bacchae") present two scenes from the world of Greek legend. *Idyll XVIII* deals with Helen's wedding with Menelaus; the poem purports to be the marriage song or epithalamium which the maidens of Sparta once sang outside the bridal chamber. It reflects the ritualized banter to which Greek newlyweds were subjected by their friends, both at night after the groom had locked himself in with the bride, and early the next morning when the couple were again disturbed by boisterous singing and dancing (cf. the *diergetikon* of lines 55 - 57).[47]

Idyll XXVI tells the story of Pentheus' death at the hands of his frenzied mother Agaue and her sister Ino and Autonoe; all three had been driven mad by the god Dionysos, who took terrible revenge for the persecution which Pentheus had visited upon him. Dover's introduction to the poem cites parallels with Euripides' account of the same gruesome event in his tragedy *The Bacchae*. The farewell to Dionysos (33 - 38) is hymnlike. *Idyll XXVI*, which is not a very interesting poem in itself, was perhaps commissioned for a Ptolemaic festival in honor of Dionysos (cf. Athenaeus V. 196 - 203); in similar fashion, the *Adonia* described in *Idyll XV* included specially commissioned works of art and poetry as well as ritual and pageantry.

Various epigrams have been ascribed to Theocritus. Those numbered 1 - 22 seem most likely to be authentic, and also appear in the *Palatine Anthology*. *Epigrams 1 - 6* contain pastoral motifs easily recognized as Theocritean—and easily imitated. *Epigram 4*, which is more an elegy than an epigram, has a special ring of authenticity to it, with its pleas to Priapus to cure the poet of his infatuation with a boy, combined with an even more ardent request for the phallic godling to grant him success in his amorous undertaking; the parallels with *Idyll XXX* are obvious. *Epigram 9* purports to be the epitaph of a fellow Syracusan expatriate who, like Elpenor in *Book X* of the *Odyssey*, died while drunk and was buried in foreign soil. A group of five epigrams honors various poets: Anacreon *(17)*, the Syracusan comic poet Epicharmus *(18)*, Hipponax *(19)*, Archilochus *(21)* and Pisander *(22)*.

CHAPTER 4

The Literary Background of the Idylls

THEOCRITUS began his career as a poet in the first quarter of the third century B.C.—that is, after a glorious period of almost five hundred years during which most of the Greek literary masterpieces which we study, admire, and enjoy today had found their first audiences. Thanks to the labors of the scholar-poets of the Alexandrian world, beginning with Theocritus' teacher Philetas of Cos, most of this impressive literary heritage was available to him—if only at the Library in Alexandria. It is thus hardly surprising that Theocritus' poetry, like the poetry of his Alexandrian contemporaries, echoes at times with the themes, motifs, and turns of phrase of earlier Greek literature.

Students of Theocritus have found Gow's detailed commentary to be an excellent guide to the literary background of the *Idylls*, and only a commentary of such generous length could do justice to the many problems which arise in judging the relationship of a turn of phrase, motif, image or narrative outline to earlier Greek literary sources or parallels. Gow's notes should be supplemented with Dover's notes, more recent scholarship, and, it is necessary to add, a desire to grasp the original poetic intention of Theocritus.

One example will have to do. In *Idyll XI* ll. 17 - 18 Theocritus describes Polyphemus "sitting on a high rock and looking out to sea." Gow would have us see in these lines a reminiscence of *Odyssey V* ll. 156 - 57, where Odysseus, held captive by the nymph Calypso on her island, pines away with longing for his home across the seas:

> . . . he sat on the rocky shore
> and broke his own heart groaning, with eyes wet
> scanning the bare horizon of the sea."
> (translated by Robert Fitzgerald)

113

Polyphemus, however, is not weeping; rather, by taking up his position on the high rock, he has raised his spirits as well, as it were. The phrase in *Idyll XI* l. 18 *es ponton horōn* ("looking out to sea") is actually closer to the phrase *horoōn ep'apeirona ponton* in *Iliad I* ll. 349 - 50, where Achilles, whose love Briseis has been taken from him by Agamemnon, is described as follows:

> . . . Achilleus
> weeping went and sat in sorrow apart from his companions
> beside the beach of the grey sea looking out on the
>   infinite water.
> (translated by Richmond Lattimore)

If Achilles is looking out to sea, it is because his mother Thetis, whom he is about to address, is a sea-dwelling Nereid; Polyphemus looks seawards, since he too is about to address a Nereid. So far, so good. But the question remains to be answered whether the comparison of Odysseus and/or Achilles with the Theocritean Cyclops was worth making in the first place? Do we really expect that Theocritus intended his audience to make something of the matter, or not? I suspect not, and I suspect that Gow did not expect it either, which is why his remark that "Theocritus is probably conscious also of Odysseus on Calypso's island—Od. 5.156"[1] means little; Theocritus may have been conscious of this and several other things as well, but *Idyll XI* is anything but a record of his private stream of consciousness.

The excursus that we have just made into the briarpatch of traditional commentary has been useful, I believe, in establishing three points which should be kept in mind when approaching the problem of sources, antecedents, parallels, etc. First of all, much of Greek literature has been lost; given the absence of many potential sources, or their survival in only fragmentary form, it is frequently impossible to judge exactly how much literary indebtedness Theocritus incurs in the *Idylls*. Second, the Alexandrian period enjoyed learned references and the reworking of older themes, it is true; but the art of literary reminiscence was, at least with the best poets, a subtle and sophisticated procedure, and should be studied as such—that is, one should endeavor to elucidate the original poetic intention, if one's remarks are to have any critical value. Finally, attention must be given to the exact wording of a Greek passage cited as a source or inspiration, since there is no other way to determine whether an allusion is being made or whether there is simply an accidental similarity of expression; there are, after all, only so many ways of saying "looking out to sea."

I Earlier Greek Literature and Pastoral

Much speculation has been made about the origins of Greek pastoral poetry. Was Theocritus its creator? Or did Theocritus draw heavily on pastoral motifs and themes which he found in earlier Greek literature? Both questions deserve to be answered in the affirmative, as we shall see. There is hardly a single motif or theme in Theocritus' pastoral poetry which does not have its roots in earlier literature, and yet it is equally true that nothing like Theocritus' *Pastoral Idylls* had ever been written before. In this section, we shall examine five dimensions of the Herdsman-Poet figure (the key element of Theocritean pastoral) in order to back up this paradoxical assertion: the herdsman as a figure described with a certain amount of realism, the herdsman as lover, the herdsman as rural musician and player of the syrinx, the herdsman as rustic singer, and the herdsman as poet.

Homer's *Odyssey* provides several vividly realistic portraits of all four categories of herdsmen and their life in the ancient world. Eumaeus the swineherd is one of the key figures of the *Odyssey* from *Book XIV* onwards; however, there are no swineherd protagonists in the *Pastoral Idylls*. Eumaeus, interestingly enough, was actually the son of a landowner, and only became a swineherd after he had been abducted by Phoenician seafarers and sold as a slave to Odysseus' father Laertes (*XV* ll. 403 ff.). It is possible that Homer sees his noble background as accounting for his innate courtesy and hospitality; if so, the Renaissance tradition of the noble in pastoral exile has a distant origin indeed. Odysseus treats him as a social equal, in spite of his low status as swineherd and slave. Along with Philoetius the cowherd, who plays an important if not major role in the last books of the *Odyssey* (from *XX* l. 185 on), Eumaeus helps Odysseus defeat the suitors of Penelope and regain his rightful kingdom of Ithaca.

The Cyclops Polyphemus appears in *Book IX* of the *Odyssey* as a man-eating monster who also exercises the peaceful profession of shepherd. His portrait was considerably modified by Philoxenus, and it is this Sicilian version of the myth that Theocritus put to such good use in his *Pastoral Idylls*. Eumaeus, Philoetius and

Polyphemus are all mentioned by name in *Idyll XVI* ll. 53 - 55; obviously, Theocritus already was seeing Homer as a creator of pastoral protagonists when he wrote his petition to, or complaint about, Hiero II of Syracuse.

Another Homeric herdsman, this time a goatherd, is mentioned by name at the end of *Idyll V*. Melanthius was the only male servant of Odysseus to betray his master. As Stanford notes on *Odyssey XVII* l. 212, "his actions gave Greek goatherds a bad reputation for ever afterwards."

With Homer's brief account of the story of Boukolion in the sixth book of the *Iliad* (23 - 26) appears the oldest Greek literary reference to the theme of the loves of a herdsman and a nymph, a theme which finds its ultimate Theocritean expression in the treatment in the *Pastoral Idylls* of the myth of Galatea and Polyphemus. It will become an extremely important thematic strain for later European pastoral, since it links the world of the lowly herdsman to the semidivine realm of Eros, and allows the figure of the herdsman-lover to emerge.

Also in the *Iliad* appears the earliest Greek literary association of herdsmen with the music of the syrinx. Homer's description of the shield of Achilles (*XVIII* ll. 478 - 613), a magnificent work of art created by the god Hephaestus, is frequently cited as a source for later pastoral descriptions as well as the prototype for the type of *ekphrasis* represented by the description of the sculptured cup in *Idyll I*. Homer does indeed evoke a whole rural world in miniature, with farmers, reapers, a harvest festival, a vineyard, and the "Linos song" (*XVIII* ll. 569 - 72) which a boy sings to entertain those who are working at harvesting the grapes (for some strange reason, this *work* song is frequently cited as the earliest *pastoral* song). Homer also gives a dramatic description of some cowherds and their dogs attempting to save a bull from the attack of two lions (573 - 86), and a brief but lovely picture of sheepfolds and pasturelands (587 - 89). But it is the description of a scene of ambush and combat which is the most interesting from the standpoint of pastoral, since it describes, in vivid contrast with the preparations for the coming slaughter, two herdsmen playing on their pipes:

> . . . when they were come to the place that was set for
>   their ambush,
> in a river, where there was a watering place for all
>   animals,

> there they sat down in place shrouding themselves in
> the bright bronze.
> But apart from these were sitting two men to watch for
> the rest of them
> and waiting until they could see the sheep and the
> shambling cattle,
> who appeared presently, and two herdsmen went along
> with them
> playing happily on pipes. . . .
> 　　(*Iliad XVIII* ll. 520 - 26, translated by Richmond Lattimore)

The joy which the herdsmen are taking in their rustic music is part of the terrible irony of the scene: a moment later the herdsmen are massacred.

Rhesus, a tragedy attributed to Euripides which draws heavily on the *Iliad*, provides an especially haunting evocation of the sound of panpipes before dawn, when the chorus says:

> Already they are driving the sheep to pasture
> on the slopes of Mt. Ida: I hear
> the nocturnal cry of panpipes.
> 　　(*Rhesus*, ll. 551 - 53)

Thus far we have examined no instance of bucolic *song* as a specific motif in Greek literature before Theocritus, yet without song there could be no Theocritean pastoral at all. It is possible that Sicilian poets, starting with Stesichorus, were the first to elaborate on this motif, and that it was connected with the myth of the bucolic archpoet Daphnis; it is pointless to go into more detail on this matter, since the evidence is extremely scanty.[2]

However, one piece of evidence looks more promising from the standpoint of claiming a Sicilian origin for Theocritus' pastoral poetry. We have seen how the theme of a cure for love (the esthetic sublimation of the sexual instincts) pervades the *Pastoral Idylls* and indeed conditions the structure of the poetic sequence. A scholiast noted in connection with *Idyll XI* l. 1 ("There is no cure for love except the Muses") that, in Philoxenus' poem on the same subject, Polyphemus gave the dolphins a message for Galatea, in which he claimed to be soothing the pain of his love with the help of the Muses; and Plutarch (*Q. Conviv.* 1.5) has preserved a fragment of the poem which indicates exactly the same idea. The fragment cited by Athenaeus (15.692d) is perhaps the opening line of the Cyclops' song to Galatea.

In Philoxenus' treatment of the Sicilian version of the Polyphemus myth, Theocritus would have found a transparent bucolic allegory at work in which the Cyclops represented Dionysius of Syracuse, Galatea the tyrant's mistress of the same name, and Odysseus the daring poet-lover himself, who braved the tyrant's anger for the sake of the love of a human Galatea, not a Nereid. Philoxenus may have thus given to Theocritus not only the inspiration for one of the major themes of the *Pastoral Idylls*, but also an example of how allegory could be used in connection with a pastoral scene involving a singing shepherd.

There were early precedents for linking the figures of the Herdsman and the Poet—the ironic synthesis which was to create the Theocritean Herdsman-Poet figure. At the opening of the *Theogony*, Hesiod had described in a famous passage the exact circumstances under which the Muses first inspired him to become a poet:

> One day the Muses taught Hesiod to sing beautifully
> while he was shepherding his lambs under Mt. Helicon.
> And the first thing the goddesses told me was this:
> "O shepherds who dwell in the fields, you disgraces to mankind,
> you walking stomachs—
> we know how to tell many lies that sound like the truth,
> and how, when we so please, to tell the truth as well."
> Thus ready of speech spoke the daughters of mighty Zeus,
> and broke a laurel branch, and gave it to me as a staff. . . .
>   (*Theogony* ll. 22 - 30)

The contrast between the lowly shepherds and the rather sharp-tongued Muses is amusingly drawn; this humorous contrast between the humble status of the herdsman and the divine gift of song was to become an important element of the ironic perspective of the *Pastoral Idylls*. Theocritus may well have wished the reader to remember this episode when, in *Idyll VII* ll. 128 - 29, he had Lycidas give Simichidas his stick "as a present from the Muses."[3]

A recently discovered inscription on the island of Paros has revealed that the lyric poet Archilochus also claimed to have received his first inspiration from the Muses while he was driving a cow to market.[4] Since herding was traditionally seen as an occupation for the young (even the sons of the Homeric nobility were herdsmen in their youth, cf. Anchises, Paris), and since poetic genius was likely to manifest itself at an early age, the association of the Muses with the life of young herdsmen in the fields was a natural one, which Theocritus could easily make plausible as a realistic motif in the *Pastoral Idylls*.

In looking back to earlier Greek literature for the sources of Theocritean pastoral, attention must be paid to the specific *use* to which pastoral motifs were put. In the *Iliad*, for example, there are a number of pastoral similes, some of them of striking beauty:

> As when in the sky the stars about the moon's shining
> are seen in all their glory, when the air has fallen
> to stillness,
> and all the high places of the hills are clear, and
> the shoulders out-jutting,
> and the deep ravines, as endless bright air spills from
> the heavens
> and all the stars are seen, to make glad the heart of
> the shepherd. . . .
> (*Iliad VIII* ll. 555 - 59, translated by Richmond Lattimore)

But it would be an error to find in this simile an early expression of the pastoral theme of the Herdsman-Poet's delight in natural beauty as we find it in the *Pastoral Idylls* (cf. opening of *Idyll I*). Homer is not claiming that his shepherd is in an ecstasy of aesthetic contemplation, but rather (as George Soutar pointed out)[5] that he is glad that the night is too bright for sheep stealing or for sudden storms to threaten his flock—compare *Iliad IV* ll. 275 - 79:

> As from his watching place a goatherd watches a cloud
> move
> on its way over the sea before the drive of the west
> wind;
> far away though he be he watches it, blacker than pitch
> is,
> moving across the sea and piling the storm before it,
> and as he sees it he shivers and drives his flocks to
> a cavern. . . .
> (translated by Richmond Lattimore)

In both cases the Homeric herdsman has a purely practical relationship with Nature and natural beauty. In addition, the similes are used in order to provide the greatest possible effect of contrast with the wartime episodes in the context of which they occur: the watchfires of the Trojans in the first instance, and the maneuvering of the Achaean troops in the second.

Although in this search for the origins of Theocritean pastoral I have emphasized a number of pastoral motifs which occur in earlier Greek literature, the specific use of such motifs in Theocritean pastoral cannot be fully explained by reference to Homer, Hesiod or any other poet. But recently attention has turned to the prose writings of Plato, which seem to present a greater analogy with Theocritean pastoral than anything we have considered previously. Clyde Murley's article "Plato's Phaedrus and Theocritean Pastoral" was a trail-blazing piece of research, and still stands as an example of a sophisticated discussion of origins. According to Murley, "Plato presents a certain technique of nature description as a background for formal and artificial conversation" which provides "a fairly complete scheme of such *Idylls* as Theocritus VII, once we substitute ornamental prose for verse."[6] Murley's detailed comparison of the *Phaedrus* with Theocritean pastoral avoids superficial *rapprochements*, and yet it manages to suggest a connection between Plato and Theocritus which challenges earlier assumptions about the origins of Pastoral. Thomas G. Rosenmeyer, in the chapter on the origins of Theocritean pastoral in his recent book *The Green Cabinet*, gives support to Murley's conclusions when he writes, "I should argue that the very earliest occurrence of a pastoral line is in Plato's Phaedrus (241 D1) "Wolves love the lamb; so lovers crave their boy."[7]

II   *Mime, Mixture of Genres, and Myth*

It is probably the influence of Sophron, the fifth-century Syracusan creator of the literary mime, which accounts for the formal similarities between the dialogues of Plato and the *Pastoral Idylls* of Theocritus. Unfortunately, only fragments of Sophron's mimes survive. Plato admired these scenes, frequently in dialogue form, which Sophron wrote in rhythmical prose, and may have found in them the formal inspiration for his first prose dialogues which dramatized scenes from the life of his teacher Socrates. Theocritus may have found in his fellow Syracusan's occasional use of rustic protagonists (such titles as "The Tunafisher" and "The Fisherman and the Farmer" have survived) the encouragement he needed to bring herdsmen into the framework of the Hellenistic

mime, which was considered, ast least by Herondas, as a genre dealing primarily with urban life and low life.

The genre of the literary mime in Hellenistic times is linked with
the name of Herondas (or Herodas),[8] a contemporary of Theocritus
who survived only as a name until 1891, when his *editio princeps*
was published on the basis of a newly discovered papyrus. The
mime was originally a popular, subliterary genre which must have
corresponded to the modern comic skit as put on in nightclubs and
evening television shows.

In an interesting essay on the origin and development of literary
genres, David Craig listed several hypothetical laws of generic
evolution, three of which apply well enough to the genre of the
literary mime as practiced by Herondas and Theocritus:

The rise of a genre is likely to occur along with the rise of a class (e.g. in
average wealth, in the proportion of the population belonging to it).

A new genre is likely to piece itself together out of motifs, styles, means
of circulation that had belonged to some medium not thought of as art
proper.

Such an emergence is likely to take place at a time of social upheaval and
rapid change.[9]

Originally a popular genre, a subliterary form of entertainment for
the urban masses, the mime reached the peak of its literary development when it was taken up by literary artists of the caliber of
Herondas and Theocritus, at a time when the poorer free citizenry
of the Greek-speaking world was finding new and unprecedented
opportunities for economic prosperity in the empire which Alexander and his successors had won for them.

However, the literary mime was not in itself a popular genre—its
language was too artificial and "literary"—but rather represented
the result of the infiltration of popular taste into the ranks of a
highly educated and tradition-conscious intelligentsia which had
followed, like the less-educated masses, the flag of Greek hegemony
in Egypt and Asia, and had benefited from the new sources of
patronage in the cultural centers of the *oikoumenē*. There is a
special vitality in the literary mime which bears witness to the vitality of the popular genre out of which it developed—a vitality which
is lacking, for example, in the Alexandrian miniature epic, even
though the latter caters to an equally Alexandrian taste for realistic
descriptions of middle-class domestic life. A similar vogue can be
found in Hellenistic sculpture of the sort which portrayed with

great freshness of inspiration old women, beggars, and slaves.[10] This new taste for the realistic treatment of themes drawn from the life of the ordinary people of the *oikoumenē* was no doubt the result of the new spirit of social democracy which flourished paradoxically under political tyranny; the old landowning aristocracy of mainland Greece was an anachronism in the new world of the *oikoumenē*, and so was its antidemocratic system of values.

Since Theocritus and Herondas·were writing at the same time, as far as we can determine, it is hard to say whether one followed in the tracks of the other or not. But it is certainly correct to state that their approach to the genre of the mime was quite different. This is best illustrated by a comparison of Herondas' sixth and fourth mimes with Theocritus' *Idyll XV*.

Idyll XV opens with the arrival of Gorgo, who has come to chat with Praxinoa after breakfast. The scene (*XV* ll. 1 - 43) is quite lively, as Matthew Arnold emphasized in a series of exclamations ("What freedom! What animation!" etc.); but it can hardly be compared with the bawdry of the conversation between Koritto and Metro in *Mime VI* of Herondas, which revolves around the topic of a female masturbatory device *(baubōn)* which a clever cobbler makes and sells under the counter. Herondas' fourth mime, like the second part of *Idyll XV*, shows two women admiring works of art; the scene is a temple complex dedicated to the god of healing Asclepius, to whom Kynno and Kokkale have brought an offering. The mime is partly a tribute to the realistic art of the painter Apelles, and partly, like *Idyll XV*, a study of the impact of art on alert but unsophisticated minds—a theme inspired by the socially democratic spirit of the *oikoumenē*. But *Idyll XV* contains a striking if typically Theocritean addition to the stock devices of the urban mime: the hymn to Adonis which, for all its parodistic overtones, represents that element of *song* which distinguishes Theocritus' mimes from those of Herondas, and which becomes the centerpiece in most of the pastoral idylls.

It is a commonplace to maintain that Hellenistic poets achieved whatever degree of originality with which they may be credited through the mixture of traditional literary genres. This mixture of genres is clearly discernible in the urban and pastoral mimes of Theocritus. *Idyll XV*, as we have just seen, is a literary mime to which Theocritus has joined a subtle parody of an Alexandrian hymn. This insertion of *song* into the context of *mime* is to be found in all of Theocritus' mimes, pastoral as well as nonpastoral, with the exception of *Idyll II* (where the incantation might be considered a form of song, however), *Idyll IV* (where song is at least mentioned), and *Idyll XIV*. The songs themselves present great generic variety: amoebaean songs in *Idylls V* and *VI*, a Daphnis song in *Idyll I*, snatches of work songs in *Idyll X*, and so on. *Narrative frames*, lacking in the mimes of Herondas, play an important role in *Idylls VI*, *VII*, and *XI*, and destroy the dramatic illusion which the mime, in its origin at least a purely dramatic form, sought to maintain.

Corresponding to the mixture of genres in the *Pastoral Idylls* is the mixed radical of presentation: narrative (the narrative frames), dramatic (the mime elements proper), and lyric (the songs). This mixed radical of presentation was to become one of the hallmarks of the pastoral genre which developed out of Theocritus' *Pastoral Idylls*. Eventually it became possible for European Pastoral to favor one radical of presentation over another and give birth to the pastoral novel, the pastoral drama and the pastoral lyric; this process of generic evolution will be examined in the last chapter of this book.

For Northrop Frye, the Greek mime was "a dead center of complete realism" which could be best described as "representing human life without comment and without imposing any sort of dramatic form beyond what is required for simple exhibition."[11] However, the most recent editor of the text of the *Mimiambi*, I. C. Cunningham, raises an important issue when he writes: "For a work of literature to be realistic in any meaningful sense, not only must the content be realistic, but the language in which it is written must be that which the characters would use in similar situations in real life."[12] Since Herondas puts a sixth-century version of the Eastern Ionic dialect into the mouths of his Hellenistic characters, it is difficult to find in his mimes a foretaste of the European realistic theater of the end of the nineteenth century. The artificial nature of Herondas' language distinguishes his literary mimes from the popular mime as well as from the mimes in prose of Sophron; the same may be said of the pastoral and nonpastoral mimes of Theocritus, although the question of language is somewhat more complicated, and will be treated in section IV of this chapter. It is enough for the moment to note that the Alexandrian who ridicules the Doric accent of Gorgo and her friend Praxinoa in *Idyll XV* ll. 87 - 88 does so in exactly the same dialect! Of course, an exact reproduction of spoken conversation (as in unedited transcriptions of taped conversations) would be intolerable even for a reader of modern novels, most of which purport to reproduce conversation realistically, but which in fact iron out or eliminate the hesitations, repetitions and parataxis which are the natural characteristics of ordinary speech. However, criteria for literary realism are relative, and a Greek reader may not have felt the use of an archaic dialect *in verse* to be as artificial as we would today.

In Frye's neo-Aristotelian terminology, the Greek mime presented its image of life in a mixture of the low mimetic and the ironic modes; that is, the reader or spectator in Hellenistic times would have felt slightly superior to the protagonists of some of Herondas' scenes from middle-class life, if only because less educated women were the protagonists, and quite superior to the protagonists of his scenes of low life, which featured pimps, slaves, etc. The same would have been true for the reader of Theocritus: any literate Greek of the *oikoumenē* would have felt superior to the herdsmen of the *Pastoral Idylls,* since herdsmen were low men on the totem pole of Hellenistic society, social exotics, anachronistic survivors of another age when stock-breeding had been the main source of wealth, and young princes herded cattle.

However, the Theocritean herdsman was, as we have seen, more than just a herdsman: he was a Herdsman-Poet, a figure who synthesized the attributes of the least literate class with those of the Hellenistic intelligentsia. Herondas' characters, by way of contrast, were no more than what they seemed to be, and the same can be said of the characters of the nonpastoral mimes of Theocritus. What accounts for the difference between pastoral and nonpastoral mimes is something that Northrop Frye considered to be a phenomenon unique to modern Western literature (especially Joyce and Kafka): "the reappearance of myth in the ironic."[13] Behind the humble figure of the Theocritean herdsman looms the myth of the Poet, a tragic myth in the case of Daphnis, a comic heroic myth in the case of Polyphemus. Both myths are in fact variations on the myth of Orpheus, who was torn apart after losing Eurydice and forswearing the love of women (cf. the situation and "sufferings" of Daphnis), but who also managed to bring back the shade of Eurydice thanks to the charm of his singing in the first and more comic half of his story. It is this presence of the myth of the poet's life which constitutes the most striking difference between the *Mimiambi* of Herondas and the *Pastoral Idylls* of Theocritus.

III   *Theocritus and His Contemporaries*

"When it comes to singing, I am still no match for the worthy Sicelidas of Samos or for Philetas—just a frog competing with grasshoppers." With these modest words *(Idyll VII* ll. 39 - 41), Theocritus mentions two of his older contemporaries by name, and praises them in a transparent pastoral allegory. Philetas, as we have seen, was one of the first scholar-poets of Hellenistic times, and had been the tutor of the young Ptolemy Philadelphus before Theocritus came to the island of Cos. Only fragments of Philetas' poetry survive, but it is easy to imagine how influential he must have been, thanks to his connections with the court at Alexandria as well as to his depth of scholarship and poetic genius. We are in a better position to assess the poetry of Sicelidas (or Asclepiades) of Samos, many of whose epigrams have survived. His poetry is unusual for its expression of wit and feeling in a simple and direct manner. Its subject matter is primarily the love of courtesans *(hetaerae).*[14]

Lycidas replies to Theocritus-Simichidas' praise of Asclepiades and Philetas in a rather cryptic manner:

> How I hate builders who try to make houses rise
> to the height of the peak of Mt. Oromedon;
> and I hate those birds of the Muses
> who waste their energy crowing against the man from Chios.
>   (*VII* ll. 45 - 48)

The passage is commonly taken to mean that Lycidas (and by implication, Theocritus himself) felt that it was impossible to rival Homer (the bard of Chios), and that the modern, that is, Alexandrian poet's chance of success lay with the smaller forms of poetry, and not with the epic or the longer forms.

Callimachus was the most vocal defender of this Alexandrian taste for the miniature in literature, and the prologue of his *Aetia* is the most impressive statement of his position which has survived. The following two lines, later imitated by Virgil in *Eclogue VI* ll. 3 - 5, purport to be the words of Apollo, and present Callimachus' poetic credo in a nutshell:

> Singer, fatten the animal for sacrifice as much as you can,
> but keep your Muse nice and thin.
>   (*Aetia I* ll./ 23 - 24)

Since Theocritus' *Idylls* are certainly the finest inspirations of the
slender Alexandrian Muse, it is usually assumed that, through the
words of Lycidas in *Idyll VII* ll. 45 - 48, Theocritus was publicly
declaring his adherence to the Callimachean principles of literary
composition.

Callimachus, like Theocritus, was an expatriate from a Dorian
city (Cyrene, on the coast of Libya) who eventually found a patron
in Ptolemy Philadelphus (cf. *Hymn IV* ll. 160 ff. and *Idyll XVII* ll.
58 ff.).[15] He was associated with the Library, and compiled the
Pinakes, a *catalogue raisonné* which was a pioneering work in the
field of literary history. He was a scholarly poet with a charming
sense of humor; I have already quoted his witty response to
Theocritus' "cure for love" topos in *Idyll XI* (see Chapter 2, section
VII).

Callimachus' approach to the problems of writing epic narrative
without crowing against the bard of Chios may have inspired
Theocritus' poems on epic themes, especially *Idyll XXIV* ("The Little Heracles"). In Callimachus' *Hecalē*, which dealt with the theme
of Theseus and the Marathonian bull, the heroic side of Theseus'
adventure was apparently subordinated to the evocation of the old
woman Hecale, in whose humble dwelling the mighty hero deigned
to take refuge. This "domestication" of heroic themes is part of the
shift in Alexandrian literature from high mimetic to low mimetic
and ironic narrative modes, and corresponds to the decline of
aristocratic standards in literature, at a time when the position of
the traditional landed aristocracy was being taken by the newly
prosperous middle classes who formed the social backbone of the
Greek cities founded by Alexander and his successors.

Callimachus mentions Theocritus by name in one of his epigrams
(LIII), and in another *(XXIV)*, he pays tribute to the vogue of
pastoral which Theocritus' *Pastoral Idylls* had started in Alexandria:

> Astacides the Cretan goatherd was abducted by a Nymph
> from the hill, and now he is worshipped as a hero.
> No more shall we shepherds sing of Daphnis
> in the shade of Dictaean oaks, but only of Astacides.

The motif of the Daphnis song is taken straight from Theocritus, in
all likelihood; and the abduction of a goatherd by a Nymph reflects
the general theme of the loves of a herdsman and a Nymph which is

found throughout the *Pastoral Idylls* as well as the fate of Hylas in *Idyll XIII.*

However, pastoral motifs had been used in lyric poetry before Theocritus. Anyte, a poetess of the early third century B.C. like Theocritus came from an area (Arcadia) traditionally associated with the songs of herdsmen, and wrote in Doric dialect. The following epigram is worth quoting, since Webster finds in it "the beginning of pastoral poetry":[16]

> Stranger, rest your weary limbs under the elm;
> sweetly murmurs the wind in the green leaves.
> Drink cool water from the spring. Travellers
> love this spot on a hot summer day.

Such epigrams perhaps prepared the way for Theocritus' later success at the Ptolemaic court in Alexandria, although it is unfair to see in their mere use of pastoral motifs the origin of Theocritean pastoral poetry, which is characterized above all by the presence of the Herdsman-Poet, a figure who is totally absent from this epigram and others like it.

The influence which folk songs and poetry had on some of the European Romantic movements can be documented; and it is possible and even likely that, to some extent, Theocritus based his pastoral poetry on the actual songs of the Greek herdsmen of his day. It is hard to account for his stylistic use of repetition, refrain, and amoebaean exchange in any other way. However, the question will probably remain moot, unless some collection of Hellenistic herdsmen's songs miraculously surfaces from the sands of Egypt. In the meantime, the following modern song will have to serve as an example of what herdsmen's songs *might* have been like in the time of Theocritus. It was sung by a Greek shepherd of Kalymnos, accompanied by his son on the tsambouna or bagpipes, and is titled "The Shepherd and the King" (*"Ho Boskos ki ho Basilias"*); in it a king and a shepherd lay a wager, the shepherd's sheep against the king's own wife:

> "Now you tell me, good shepherd,
> what will you wager?"
> "I'll wager a thousand sheep
> with silver bells
> and my best lamb
> with the silklike wool."

When the shepherd
brought his sheep,
the shepherd brought his sheep
down to the watering place,
the queen appeared
at a far-off window:
"I wish I were a shepherdess
and cheesemaker
so I could hear the birds singing in the *mandri*
and make fresh cheese."
        (recorded, transcribed, and translated by Ellen Frye)[17]

In this modern song an actual herdsman sings about a legendary
herdsman and a king; in *Idyll VII*, Lycidas sang about Comatas and
the evil tyrant. The simple pastoral life is praised by an actual
shepherd-singer, just as it was by Theocritus' herdsman-poets; the
song celebrates a world of singing birds, sheep-pens *(mandri)*, and
cheesemaking which is reminiscent of the world of the *Pastoral
Idylls*—compare the song of the Cyclops in *Idyll XI*, especially lines
34 - 49, for the motif of pastoral wealth, and lines 63 - 66, which
offer a striking parallel to the words of the queen at the end of the
modern Greek song, where, however, the "come live with me and
be my love" *topos* is changed to "I wish I could come live with you
and be your love."

Apollonius ("of Rhodes") was the only major Alexandrian poet to
be born in the city of Alexandria. His romantic epic *The Voyage of
Argo (Argonautica)* was the most serious attempt on the part of a
Hellenistic "bird of the Muses" to "crow against the bard of
Chios." Virgil was certainly encouraged by his daring; his portrait
of the impassioned queen Dido in Book IV of the *Aeneid* was partially inspired by Apollonius' magnificent narration of Medea's love
at first sight for Jason in *Book III* of the *Argonautica*. Simaetha,
Theocritus' impassioned would-be sorceress, mentions the name of
Medea *(Idyll II* l. 16); Gow writes that "the third book of the
Argonautica and this Idyll are the chief surviving specimens of the
intimate analytical handling of love themes which is agreed to have
been the most important legacy of the Alexandrians to European
poetry."[18]

It is generally assumed that Apollonius and Callimachus were at
each other's throats over the question of the relevance of the
Homeric epic as a model for Hellenistic poetry. Callimachus ap-

parently felt that long poems were out of the question; Apollonius disagreed. Since Theocritus apparently took the side of Callimachus, scholars have been eager to see in *Idylls XIII* and *XXII*, in which Theocritus treated material which Apollonius also treated in the *Argonautica* (*Book I* ll. 1207 ff. for the Hylas episode, Book *II* ll. 1 - 97 for Polydeuces' fight with Amycus), illustrations of the artistic consequences of this Alexandrian battle of the books. Gow has argued that Theocritus rehandled Apollonius' material in order to bring his versions more in line with the Callimachean *ars poetica;*[19] Webster is less impressed with the evidence for a Theocritean onslaught on poor Apollonius;[20] Dover is willing to grant Gow this point, but adds, "Which of the two poets has handled the theme[s] better is a matter on which readers disagree."[21] Readers might at least agree that the problem has all the makings of a perfect scholarly controversy, since there is no way to settle the issue short of an accurate dating of the various stages of composition of the *Argonautica* and of the two idylls of Theocritus in question—and such accurate dating is, fortunately or unfortunately, impossible.

The question of the relationship of Theocritus' poetry, and especially his pastoral poetry, to the visual art of his time has been carefully examined by T. B. L. Webster in *Hellenistic Poetry and Art* and *The Age of Hellenism.*[22] Webster examines, as does Lawall, herdsman-satyr figures in the plastic arts.[23] He also deals with the difficult question of the relationship of the poetic *locus amoenus* to its analogues in the visual arts. According to Webster, the artistic motif of the vineclad grotto of the Nymphs and Dionysus was the source of Theocritus' pastoral scenes, and also inspired the artificial bowers constructed for drinking parties. If Webster's hypothesis is correct, then it helps account for the use in Theocritean pastoral of motifs of symposiastic origin (the *kōmos,* "symptoms of love," Lycidas' rustic *symposion* in *Idyll VII,* etc.), since the pastoral landscape would have readily suggested the idea of a drinking party. The realistic depiction of children (cf. *Idyll XXIV* "The Little Heracles"), or old people (cf. the old fisherman on the cup in *Idyll I*), and of domestic animals (throughout the *Pastoral Idylls*), and more generally what Margarete Bieber[24] has called "Rococo trends in Hellenistic art," presents obvious analogies with Theocritus' literary art, although the question of the *significance* of these analogies is still a matter for further research to uncover.

IV   *Language, Style, and Verse*

The seven *Pastoral Idylls* as well as the four mimes of Theocritus were written in a predominantly Doric dialect of Greek. The poems to patrons and the poems on epic themes mix epic-Ionic and Doric dialects, with the exception of *Idyll XXII*, which, like *Idyll XII*, is in pure epic-Ionic. All of the poems just mentioned are in hexameters. "The Distaff" *(Idyll XXVIII)* and the two remaining poems on paederastic love *(Idylls XXIX* and *XXX)* resurrect the old Aeolic dialect and meters of Sappho and Alcaeus. Most of the epigrams are in Doric elegiacs.

So much for the bare linguistic facts of the matter. What do we make of them? The closest imitation of Theocritus' pastoral language in English might be found in Spenser's *Shepheardes Calender;* John Dryden thought so, at any rate, and considered Theocritus' Doric a perfect model for rustic speech: "The boorish dialect of Theocritus has a secret charm in it which the Roman language cannot imitate. But Spenser, being master of our northern dialect, and skilled in Chaucer's English, has . . . exactly imitated the Doric of Theocritus."[25] Gow is willing to grant the traditional point that Theocritus' Doric had some flavor of rusticity for a third-century audience (the *koinē* or standard Greek of the Macedonian kingdoms was basically Attic), but he goes on to give a philologically more sophisticated picture of the language of the *Pastoral Idylls* and the mimes:

Theocritus's dialect is artificial, peculiar to himself, and not consistent even in his own usage. He is not writing his native Syracusan, nor is he imitating those who had written it before him (Epicharmus and Sophron, for instance) as in the Aeolic poems he imitates Sappho and Alcaeus. . . . As Burns modified his native Ayrshire dialect with words drawn both from other parts of Scotland and from literature, so Theocritus, but much more freely.[26]

But Dover plays down the element of artificiality which Gow wants to stress: "Perhaps as many as half the words in Theocritus which seem to us 'poetic' when we consider them from an Attic standpoint were not so from a Dorian standpoint" and would have been everyday language for a Doric-speaking Syracusan or Coan.[27] In addition, a literate Alexandrian Greek was perfectly used to Homeric language (epic-Ionic), and had a higher tolerance for deviation in poetry from the contemporary spoken norms than we do today, influenced as we are by William Carlos Williams and the American art of plain speaking. I suspect that the actual effect of Theocritus' poetic language on his audience resembled, from the standpoint of archaism, the effect of John Barth's *The Sot-Weed Factor* on contemporary American readers, and that the Doricisms were no more exotic for non-Doric speakers than the various dialects used by Mark Twain in *Huckleberry Finn* were for its original audience.

The style of Theocritus in his *Pastoral Idylls* is admirably suited to his bucolic subject matter. The use of repetition is especially sophisticated since it aims at an effect of artless simplcity which is in fact completely calculated. The use of refrain and amoebaean exchange is, as we have seen, probably borrowed directly from sub-literary genres, perhaps from actual herdsmen's songs. Dover's edition contains an excellent analysis of Theocritus' style which even the Greekless reader will find of value.

The music of Theocritus' verse is something that is within the powers of practically any reader to appreciate, even if his Greek is less than Shakespeare's. It is a style which has immediate appeal; in classical times the critic Hermogenes called it "smooth," and Demetrius mentioned its "sweetness." This sweet musicality is based on a very marked preference for alliteration and assonance, which creates a continual echoing of sounds, and thus dampens potentially harsh effects; it frequently results from the close repetition of words and parallel constructions. The most noteworthy feature of Theocritus' Doric, the broad "a" sound (which replaces the Attic "ē"), is used to smooth out vowel coloring. The total effect of Theocritus' verse music in the *Pastoral Idylls* is unique in Greek literature.

According to Legrand,[28] this strong musicality may have resulted from the fact that Theocritus' poetry (along with most scholarly Alexandrian verse) was intended for reading only. Deprived of traditional musical accompaniment and recitation, the Alexandrians were led to compose with more regard for the inner ear. The quite obvious and strong effects of Theocritus' verse may well owe a good deal to this absence of the traditional lyric radical of presentation. In addition, since Theocritus' herdsmen are frequently supposed to be singing, something was certainly needed to inject this absent but imagined music into their hexameters. The verse itself trips along in a lively manner, dactyl after dactyl. It is often interrupted by a strong pause before the fifth foot (the so-called "bucolic dieresis") which gives a peculiarly rhythmic swing to this bucolic version of the Homeric meter of epic recitation.

CHAPTER 5

The Influence of Theocritus

THE influence of Theocritus' poetry on the course of Western literature is a topic for a lengthy study by itself, for no other Greek author was as often imitated and as successfully imitated at times as Theocritus. However, two basic points should be kept in mind: Theocritus influenced Western literature primarily through Virgil's reworking of the themes and motifs of the *Pastoral Idylls* in the *Eclogues;* and his direct influence can be traced as a rule only in the works of those poets (Virgil, Sannazaro, Ronsard, Milton, Gnedich, Arnold, et al.) who knew enough Greek to read him in the original.

Theocritus' *Pastoral Idylls* created a new literary genre, and individual idylls became the prototypes for its various forms: *Idylls III* and *XI* for the pastoral monologue, *Idyll V* for amoebaean song, etc. Such a great quantity of mediocre verse in the pastoral vein exists that scholars and critics tend to forget that the pastoral tradition which Theocritus' *Pastoral Idylls* initiated also inspired a few undisputed masterpieces of European literature: Virgil's *Eclogues,* Garcilaso's three eclogues in Spanish, Tasso's Italian pastoral play *Aminta,* Milton's "Lycidas," and *L'Après-midi d'un faune* of the French poet Mallarmé. These and other less celebrated works of European Pastoral attest to the formal influence of the *Pastoral Idylls* and to the perennial fascination of the world of herdsmen-poets and herdsmen-lovers to which the imagination of Theocritus gave birth.

I *Imitation of Theocritean Motifs*

The influence of Theocritus is most easily seen in the frequent and close imitation of Theocritean motifs by later poets working in the pastoral tradition. Such a frequent and close imitation of motifs is the most constant feature of European pastoral poetry, which developed as the result of an unusually deliberate process of assimilation and imitation of earlier models. One example will have to do. In *Idyll VI* ll. 34 - 39 the one-eyed Cyclops Polyphemus remembers a moment of comic narcissistic self-admiration:

> Actually, I am not as bad-looking as people say I am.
> The other day I looked at my reflection in the sea—the
>   sea was calm—
> and my beard looked good, my one and only eyeball looked
>   good,
> —as far as I could tell—and my teeth
> gleamed whiter and brighter than Parian marble.

With his single eye in the middle of his forehead, and the single shaggy eyebrow above it, the young Cyclops could easily think of himself as a freak, unless he made, as he did, a determined effort to find himself attractive.

In Virgil's imitation of the same motif in *Eclogue II* ll. 25 - 27, a certain amount of the humor is lost, since the shepherd Corydon does not have the Cyclops' reasons for being afraid of being called an ugly freak by his neighbors:

> nec sum adeo informis: nuper me in litore vidi,
> cum placidum ventis staret mare; non ego Daphnim
> iudice te metuam, si numquam fallit imago.

> Nor am I as ill-favoured as all that. Down by the sea the
> other day, I saw myself reflected when the dying wind had
> left the water calm. You could compare me even with Daphnis,
> and I should have no fears—if mirrors do not lie.
>   (translated by E. V. Rieu)

Ronsard's poem *Le Cyclope Amoureux* (The Cyclops in Love) is probably the best of the Renaissance imitations of *Idyll XI* which stay close enough to the original to qualify, at least by Renaissance standards, as translations. Yet, although Ronsard's poem is an expansion of the Greek model for his eclogue (306 lines, as opposed to 81 for *Idyll XI*), the motif of *Idyll VI* ll. 34 - 39, included here through the process of *contaminatio* (see Section II), seems unexpectedly compressed:

Certes je me cognois, je ne suis si difforme
Qu'en beauté je ne trouve agréable ma forme:

> Ma face l'autre jour dans l'onde j'esprouvay,
> Quand la Mer estoit calme, et beau je me trouvay.

> Indeed I know myself, and am not so misshapen
> That with my own beauty I cannot be taken.
> Th'other day in the sea at my image I gazed
> When the water was calm, and my beauty I praised.
>   (ll. 273 - 76)

In fact, Ronsard is not imitating Theocritus but rather Ovid's imitation of the Theocritean motif in the *Metamorphoses* (*Met. XIII* ll. 840 - 41):

> Certe ego me novi liquidaeque in imagine vidi
> Nuper aquae placuitque mihi mea forma videnti.

> Indeed I know myself; the other day I saw myself reflected
>   in the water,
> and as I gazed, I grew pleased with my beauty.

The following quotation from Marvell's "Damon the Mower" demonstrates that wit and ingenuity had their place in the process of introducing traditional Theocritean motifs into European pastoral poetry. Since the speaker is equipped with a scythe, it is only natural for him to gaze at his reflection in its polished surface:

> Nor am I so deformed to sight
> If in my scythe I looked right;
> In which I see my picture done,
> As in a crescent moon the sun.
>   (ll. 57 - 60)

To go on simply listing the various imitations of Theocritean motifs would quickly degenerate into a pedant's game of source-hunting or *Quellenforschung*. What is important to grasp is the way in which these motifs were *used* by various poets working in the Western pastoral tradition, starting with Virgil.

II *Virgil*

Theocritus' *Idylls* had some impact on later Greek poetry, if we can judge by the little which survives of what might have been a harvest of Greek bucolic verse of the later Alexandrian period.

Bion's "Lament for Adonis" must have been inspired by the hymn to Adonis in *Idyll XV* as well as by the use of refrain in *Idylls I* and *II*. The "Lament for Bion" was partly modelled after the lament for Daphnis in *Idyll I;* it became the prototype for the European pastoral elegy.[1] The *pseudo-Theocritea*—works once attributed to Theocritus but now generally considered to be by imitators, although they still retain their numbering as *Idylls*—were frequently imitated by later poets (*Idylls VIII, IX,* and *XXVII* especially), and several probably were already associated with the genuine poems of Theocritus when they were included in an anthology of bucolic verse edited by the grammarian Artemidorus (first century B.C.). This was presumably the edition which Virgil pored over while he was composing his *Eclogues*. A late but significant witness to the reputation of Theocritus throughout antiquity is to be found in the pastoral color and style of *Daphnis and Chloe*, (*c.* A.D. 200), a prose work by Longus[2] which deserves to be called the prototype of the Renaissance pastoral romance.

But without Virgil's Latin imitations of the *Pastoral Idylls* and the mimes, it is fair to say that the poetry of Theocritus would not have had the influence on Western literature that we are tracing. The *Eclogues* were the vehicle by means of which the forms and motifs of Theocritean pastoral poetry were passed on as one of the chief legacies of Classical literature to modern European literature. Yet even though they incorporated and preserved a vast amount of Theocritean material, the *Eclogues* of Virgil are above all an original work of the Roman poetic genius; it is as if a Greek temple had been dismantled and a Roman villa constructed out of its materials.

A rough idea of how Virgil proceeded to change a Theocritean idyll (or several Theocritean idylls) into a Latin eclogue can be gotten by examining the way Virgil used *Idyll XI*. Cartault compiled the following list of Virgilian borrowings: XI.19 (Theocritus) to II.6 (Virgil); XI.20 f. to VII.37 f.; XI.25 f. to VIII.37 f.; XI.29 to II.6; XI.31 f. to VIII.34; XI.34 f. to II.21 f.; XI.38 f. to II.23 f.; XI.40 f. to II.40 f.; XI.42 to II.45; XI.42f. to IX.39; XI.51 to VII.49; XI.56 f. to II.45 f.; XI.65 to II.28 f.; XI.72 f. to II.69 f.[3] It should be clear from this list that Virgil got most of his materials for *Eclogue II* from *Idyll XI*, although one should add that he borrowed from *Idylls III* (along with *Idyll XI*, the model for the type of pastoral monologue of which *Eclogue II* is the first Latin example), *VI, VII,* and *X* as well; and that *Idyll XI* was also put to use when Virgil composed *Eclogues VII*, *VIII*, and *IX*.

This process of using several sources in order to create a new poem ought to have a name. The term *contaminatio*, originally used to designate the process through which Terence borrowed elements from two or more Greek plays for one of his Roman comedies, fits Virgil's procedure in most of his eclogues, and is an even more useful term when applied to the Humanistic poetry of the Renaissance, a period when literary borrowings were a sign that a scholar-poet knew his classical authors. Pastoral poets starting with Virgil made *contaminatio* into a standard feature of the European eclogue.[4]

It is immediately noticeable from Cartault's list that Virgil did not use all of *Idyll XI* in his *Eclogues*. Although he used the greater part of the song of Polyphemus in *Idyll XI* (19 - 79) as material for his *Eclogues* and for *Eclogue II* in particular, he seems to have found no use at all for the motivating idea of the narrative frame (*Idyll XI* ll. 1 - 18 and 80 - 81) which is of such crucial importance for the understanding of Theocritus' last pastoral idyll. Indeed, one is forced to conclude that Virgil deliberately avoided any mention of the Theocritean idea that poetry can be a cure for love. This discovery enables us to understand how *Eclogue II* differs radically from its Theocritean model.

In *Eclogue II*, the shepherd Corydon (a name borrowed from *Idyll III*) is desperately in love—a situation which Theocritus dramatized with the lovelorn Cyclops in *Idyll XI*. But Corydon is no mythic Cyclops, and his love is no Nereid but a boy, Alexis, whose favors have been bought by Iollas, the wealthy farmer who presumably owns Alexis as a slave. Corydon, who is perhaps a slave himself, is in no position to compete with Iollas for the favors of Alexis; indeed, Alexis cares nothing for a mere shepherd's gifts, since Iollas can always offer more (56 - 57). All Corydon can offer is his songs, but Alexis (like Galatea in *Idyll XI* and Amaryllis in *Idyll III*) cares nothing for them (6).

The context of *Idyll XI* was mythological; in *Eclogue II*, the situation is delineated in terms of greater social realism. Alexis is no figment of Corydon's imagination (Galatea, in contrast, appeared only in the dreams of Polyphemus in *Idyll XI*), and Corydon, unlike Polyphemus, is no archetypal pastoral poet, although he would like to pass as one. Corydon's world is no landscape of the mind, but an all too confining spot in the social structure of the Italy of Virgil's time. Corydon gazes across an unbridgeable gap; but it is not the gap which lies between the real and the imagined (the girls of Sicily, and the dreamlike Galatea, for Polyphemus), but the social abyss which separates him from the wealthy Iollas. It is this particular social and economic disparity which puts Corydon's plight far beyond the cure of song.

Thus Corydon is a more romantic and tragic figure than Polyphemus. Virgil has deliberately toned down the comic-ironic dimension of the Theocritean model, and has made his herdsman protagonist the vehicle of a very different theme, which is the tragic-romantic counterpart of the comic Theocritean theme—at least, up to a point. Toward the end of the eclogue, Virgil gives to Corydon two lines of seemingly great tragic intensity: noticing how the sun is going down, and the shadows are lengthening, Corydon complains that his love, unlike the sun, has lost none of its power to burn:

> me tamen urit amor; quis enim modus adsit amori?
> A Corydon, Corydon, quae te dementia cepit?
> (68 - 69)

> But love scorches me all the same: is there then no
> limit to love?
> Ah Corydon, Corydon! What madness has seized you?

But Corydon is hardly capable of bearing the burden of tragedy for long—line 69 is in fact a paraphrase of Theocritus *XI* l. 72 ("O Cyclops, Cyclops—where have your wits flown away to?"). It leads to a comic reversal of the situation, which is perhaps not altogether satisfactory from the standpoint of motivation (certainly not when compared with the corresponding reversal in *Idyll XI*), since we wonder how the hot fire of love can be so easily quenched: "You will find another Alexis, if this one disdains you" (73, *invenies alium, si te hic fastidit, Alexin*). In spite of his occasionally romantic utterances, Corydon is a *rusticus* (56), a basically comic figure, a sad clown.

But even a rustic's love can have tragic overtones which transcend the power of pastoral poetry to allay. No act of the imagination can quite conceal the fact that Corydon's frustration reveals to him the pain of life in a world where social injustice and inequality are the natural features of the pastoral social landscape. The

Theocritean Cyclops in his mythological Sicilian landscape was, of course, a stranger to such a realistic vision.

Virgil imitated the general pattern of the song of Polyphemus as it is found in *Idyll XI* of Theocritus, but studiously avoided any restatement of the idea which motivated it, because he wished to use the figure of a rustic lover not only for comic and ironic purposes, but also as a vehicle for the tragic and romantic theme of social injustice which played such an important role in the *Eclogues*—a theme totally absent from the *Pastoral Idylls*. *Eclogue II* continues the theme of *Eclogue I*, where the sufferings of the unfortunate Meliboeus (whose lands have been confiscated) are in no was cured or mitigated by the songs of the more fortunate and leisured Tityrus. Virgil's *Eclogue II*, by maintaining Corydon in his ambiguous posture (midway between Meliboeus and Polyphemus, as it were), maintains the tension between two opposing themes: the world of social injustice, and the "play" of art.

Thus *Eclogue II* deliberately avoids explicit thematic unity—unlike *Idyll XI* and its single interpretive frame of reference. *Eclogue II* is a good example of Virgil's artistic practice in the realm of pastoral in that, for all its Theocritean touches, it remains faithful to the dual task which Virgil set for his Eclogue Book as a whole: to reflect the world of the mind (the literary Arcadia of neoteric poetry, the Theocritean pastoral patrimony) as well as the political and social world of Rome.

It cannot be denied that Virgil significantly enlarged the scope of the Theocritean pastoral idyll, frequently to the point where the "counterforce" (the impingement of the wider world of history and politics) appears to be more important than the idyllic vision itself.[5] In fact, he does this from the very first lines of *Eclogue I*, where the leisure of Tityrus almost cries out for a justification in the face of the desperate plight of Meliboeus, whose farm has been handed over to a veteran of the civil wars. (Meliboeus embodies a plea for social justice quite alien to the poetry of Theocritus.) Tityrus' justification, such as it is, is imperial patronage: "a god provided these leisures for us" (*Eclogue I* l. 6). Tityrus is expressing allegorically Virgil's gratitude to Augustus in flattering words of the sort Theocritus had avoided in his *Pastoral Idylls*. But this kind of tribute to a patron's generosity is not really out of place in the *Eclogues*, since their major point is to bring the wider world of politics into conflict with this type of pastoral leisure, and ultimately to opt for the wider world.

For Brooks Otis, this expansion of a Theocritean kernel according to such a new schema and viewpoint is the whole "secret" of the Eclogues. Otis's remarks on Eclogue *I* ll. 40 - 41 are significant:

At no point does he abandon the bucolic manner and diction: the name Octavian or Caesar is most carefully not pronounced, but the bucolic response: "Pascite ut ante boves, pueri, submittite tauros," is enough. The deed has been done; pastoral, that most unhistorical of genres, has been Romanized and brought into history. The poet has now seen and said that poetry itself cannot live except by coming to terms with its age.[6]

Of course, there are other ways of coming to terms with an age than by dragging in major political issues in allegorical form. But in terms of the later pastoral tradition in the West, one cannot make too much of *Eclogue 1,* as Curtius is quick to point out:

From the first century of the Empire to the time of Goethe, all study of Latin literature began with the first eclogue. It is not too much to say that anyone unfamiliar with that short poem lacks one key to the literary tradition of Europe.[7]

However, it should be noted in passing (since this detail seems to have eluded the commentators) that in *Eclogue I,* at least as regards the general drift of the dialogue, Virgil owes something to Theocritus' *Idyll XIV.* This nonpastoral dialogue presents two old acquaintances, one who is ready to leave the country (Aeschinas), and the other (Thyonichus) who is ready to listen sympathetically, and who recommends Ptolemy as the finest patron a freeman could desire. Of course, it is as typical of Theocritus to attribute Aeschinas' troubles to a faithless girlfriend (this story occupies the center of this urban mime), as it is of Virgil to make Meliboeus a victim of social change. Indeed, Virgil picks up the same theme of social injustice again in *Eclogue IX;* in this darker eclogue, the older Moeris has not only been chased off the farm and almost killed by the new owner, but has lost his memory for beautiful verse as well (*Eclogue IX* l. 51: *Omnia fert aetas, animum quoque*). The eclogue is partially imitated from *Idyll VII* (Lycidas appears as an enthusiastic younger poet), but here again Theocritus' pastoral poem can claim none of the concern for social justice of Virgil's.

Idyll XI was the prototype for the most common form of pastoral monologue in the Renaissance, the pastoral love lament. Its motifs were known to most Renaissance poets, scholars, and readers through the Latin of Virgil's *Eclogue II* and the tradition of the

Virgilian eclogue, although a minority could read the actual Greek text, and an influential Latin translation of the *Idylls* by Helius Eobanus Hessus appeared in 1531. In cases where poets were not necessarily familiar with the Greek text of the Latin translation of *Idyll XI,* their use of Theocritean motifs preserved by the Virgilian tradition of pastoral is all the more interesting, since it illustrates the great indirect influence Theocritus had on Western pastoral literature.[8] A history of the use of Theocritean themes and motifs would quickly turn into a history of the pastoral genre itself.

III   *Editions, Translations, Reputation*

It is one of the ironies of literary history that it was the least Theocritean of Virgil's *Eclogues—Eclogue IV*—which guaranteed the survival of the forms, themes, and motifs of the Theocritean pastoral idyll. *Eclogue IV,* whose theme of a new Golden Age ushered in by the birth of a child was interpreted by Christians as an amazing prophecy by a pagan poet of the birth of Christ, helped give Virgil a unique place among classical authors, and sanctioned the study of his works during a Christian Dark Ages when pagan literature and learning were often somewhat suspect. With the renewal of interest in Greco-Roman culture during the Renaissance, Virgil's *Eclogues* became the ultimate source of Pastoral as practiced and understood by poets such as Spenser and Garcilaso, who probably had little if any direct contact with the actual Greek text of the *Idylls*. Of course, various Latin translations were available to them, as we shall see; and it is also possible that more learned friends were able to translate the Greek text of Theocritus for them, as Ramler was later to do for Salomon Gessner. But as a rule, it was the Virgilian tradition of the eclogue which set the tone for Renaissance Pastoral.

However, a less obvious but still important line of direct influence can be traced in the various editions, translations, and imitations of the *Idylls* from the early Renaissance onwards. From time to time the *Idylls* had an important effect on poets who could consult the text in the original. Finally, as the Virgilian tradition of the eclogue, so influential during the Renaissance, lost its prestige in the eighteenth and early nineteenth century, attention was drawn increasingly to what Theocritus had to offer as a poet in his own right—a process of reevaluation which has continued into our own time.

According to the hypothesis of Wilamowitz, the first complete edition of the *Idylls* (including idylls now considered *pseudo-Theocritea*) should be credited to Artemidorus of Tarsus, a grammarian of the first century B.C. His son Theon may have written the first commentary on Theocritus. Gow, however, finds the evidence for this "first edition" of the *Idylls* less than convincing. In fact, we know next to nothing about the early history of the text which Virgil imitated in his *Eclogues*.

Later Greek editors, inspired by the vogue of Attic Greek in the later centuries of Roman rule, probably eliminated some of the Doricisms of Theocritus' verse, but it is to them and to the long tradition of Byzantine scholarship that we owe the preservation of the *Idylls*. Byzantine manuscripts, such as the illustrated Theocritus of the Bibliothèque Nationale, where after one thousand years of Christian stewardship of pagan literature the god Pan was still represented with cloven hooves and a goat's head,[9] are the basis of modern editions of the *Idylls*, although none are earlier than the thirteenth century.

Scholia (word glosses and commentary) date back only to the tenth or eleventh century, but presumably incorporate notes of earlier commentators. The actual Byzantine manuscripts used in printing the first editions of the *Idylls* in the Renaissance were the product of a manuscript tradition which, after fifteen centuries of copying and recopying a text whose grammar and vocabulary were quite unusual, had become thoroughly contaminated. It took the labor of generations of modern editors and emendators to produce the reasonably accurate and accessible text that we find in Gow's edition of 1952.

Petrarch, the first poet to write eclogues of literary merit in modern times (*Bucolicum Carmen*, 1357), knew of Theocritus:

> . . . I recall the singer born of Sicilian
> Stock and his fellows, who, hiding in lairs from the lions,
> delighted
> In songs of the tangle-fleeced flocks that they so carefully
> guarded.
> *Eclogue* X ll. 165 - 67 (translated by Thomas G. Bergin)[10]

But since he attributed to Theocritus the use of cryptic allegory (the "lairs" which supposedly enabled Theocritus to aim political satire at the "lions" or tyrants of his day),[11] a characteristic of Petrarch's

Virgilian eclogues but one which was distinctly absent from Theocritus' *Pastoral Idylls*, it is clear that Theocritus was only a name to him. This would have been only natural, since few Western Europeans knew any Greek whatsoever from the time of the Dark Ages to the middle of the fifteenth century, and hence they had no access to the texts of the *Idylls* studied in the Greek-speaking Byzantine Empire.

Throughout the fifteenth century Byzantine manuscripts of Theocritus found their way to Italy; in 1475, the Papal Library of Sixtus IV possessed three of them.[12] They were, of course, useless until Italians began to learn enough Greek to read them. Angelo Poliziano (Politian) became the first modern Western European to achieve perfect fluency in Greek; at the age of seventeen he was already writing epigrams in Greek, and his pastoral masterpiece *Orfeo* was the result of his precocious erudition joined with poetic genius. Poliziano lectured on Theocritus in Florence during the school year 1482 - 1483, about the same time that the first printed edition *(editio princeps)* of the *Idylls* was published in Milan by Bonus Accursius. A Latin translation of *Idylls I - VII* by the Venetian scholar Phileticus followed almost immediately; the Roman edition of 1482 was reprinted in Venice in 1500 and in Paris in 1503. The beautiful Aldine edition of Theocritus (Venice, 1495) formed part of the second volume of the epoch-making series of Greek texts published by Aldus Manutius. By the beginning of the sixteenth century, the *Idylls* had once again become of major interest to scholars and poets of the Italian peninsula.

Since Latin was the *lingua franca* of the educated in Renaissance Europe, fluency in Greek being confined to a small number of serious scholars, it is reasonable to assume that acquaintance with the *Idylls* of Theocritus was most furthered by Latin translations, such as the influential version of Helius Eobanus Hessus (Basel, 1531), and by bilingual editions (Latin-Greek), such as the edition sold *ad scholas Coqueretias* in 1550, which the French humanist Jean Dorat no doubt used to instruct some of the future *Pléiade* poets at the Collège de Coqueret in Paris.[13] The traditional order of the *Idylls* (an unfortunate tradition, as we have seen) was established in 1566 by the edition of the *Idylls* contained in the *Poetae Graeci* published by Henri Estienne, who in 1579 brought out a magnificent volume *(Theocriti aliorumque poetarum idyllia)* with appendixes listing the numerous Theocritean references in Virgil and other pastoral poets.

Translation of Theocritus into the vernacular languages of Europe proceeded at a much slower pace. The *Sixe Idillia* (Anonymous) published at Oxford in 1588 included translations of only three of the authentic idylls of Theocritus (*Idylls XI, XVIII,* and *XXX*). "The Shepherds Starre" (1591) was a greatly expanded paraphrase of *Idyll III* which hardly deserves to be listed as a translation at all. The Elizabethans probably had little direct acquaintance with the pastoral poetry of Theocritus; not a single edition of the Greek text of the *Idylls* appeared in England until the seventeenth century.

Theocritus was presumably much better known in Renaissance France and Italy. Pierre de Ronsard and Antoine de Bäf were the most fervent admirers of the *Idylls*. Ronsard imitated Theocritus frequently, beginning with his imitation of *Idyll XI* in "Le Cyclope Amoureux" (1560), and Bäf published imitations of *Idylls VI, X,* and *XI*. Spenser was much indebted to the French school of pastoral poetry in his *Shepheardes Calender* (1579), and may well have absorbed the spirit of Theocritean pastoral poetry in the imitations and translations of the *Pléiade* poets. But the single most important vernacular vehicle for Theocritean themes and motifs was Jacopo Sannazaro's *Arcadia* (1504), a pastoral romance mixing prose and verse, which Jean Martin translated from the original Italian into French in 1544.

Although individual poems of Theocritus were translated now and then during the two centuries which followed the earlier editions of the Greek text of the *Idylls*, complete or nearly complete translations of the *Idylls* began to appear only towards the end of the seventeenth century: the English translation of Thomas Creech in 1684, the French translation of Longepierre in 1688, an Italian translation by Anton Maria Salvini in 1717, a Spanish translation by Juan Francisco Sandoval in 1752, and finally a German translation by S. H. Lieberkuehn in 1757. Thus until the last decade of the seventeenth century an appreciation of the *Idylls* was usually confined to a small circle of classical scholars and to an even smaller circle of Hellenists—which included, let it be emphasized, poets such as Sannazaro, Ronsard, and Milton (but not, in all likelihood, Spenser, Marvell, or Garcilaso) who read Theocritus in the original and made major contributions to the pastoral genre in their own vernacular literatures. The ordinary *reader* of Theocritus was typically someone like Fielding's character Abraham Adams in the novel *Joseph Andrews* (1742), the scholarly clergyman who read

Greek for pleasure and was able to cheer up his friend Joseph with a quote from *Idyll IV*: "He concluded with a verse out of Theocritus, which signifies no more than, That sometimes it rains, and sometimes the sun shines"[14] (cf. *Idyll IV* l. 43—Corydon cheers up Battus with the same platitude).

The name of Theocritus was traditionally linked with Virgil's in most of the earlier critical writings on Pastoral, and if preference was given to one over the other, it was usually to Virgil. However, as the Virgilian tradition of the eclogue played itself out and fell into increasing disrepute, more attention was paid to the original creator of the pastoral idyll. The publication of Ambrose Philips's eclogues in 1709 stirred up a controversy which helped to arouse critical opinion in favor of Theocritus. Partisans of Alexander Pope championed the elegance of his Virgilian pastorals and ridiculed Philips's slight attempt at Theocritean realism; but the artificiality of Virgilian pastoral had lost much of its prestige, and Theocritean realism was the wave of the future. Where once Theocritus had been criticized for his vulgarity ("Is it not true that the speeches in the *Idylls* smell too much of the countryside?" asked Fontenelle disdainfully in his *Discours sur la nature de l'églogue*), now he was praised for his naturalness and simplicity. John Gay wrote his *Shepherd's Week* (1714) as a parody of Ambrose Philips's eclogues, but readers were more inclined to ignore the parodic humor in their admiration for the realistic transposition of traditional pastoral themes and motifs to the English countryside. Gay's praise of Theocritus' rustic style was ironic ("He rightly, throughout his fifth *Idyll*, maketh his Louts give foul language, and behold their Goats at Rut in all Simplicity"),[15] but Goldsmith's later reaction to Gay's attempt at pastoral burlesque was more typical of the times: "Gay has hit the true spirit of pastoral poetry. In fact he more resembles Theocritus than any other English pastoral writer."[16] Robert Burns did no more than reflect the eighteenth century's growing preference for the vivid realism of Theocritus' pastoral mimes over the greater artificiality of the *Eclogues* of Publius Vergilius Maro, when he exclaimed:

> But thee, Theocritus, wha matches?
> They're no herd's ballats, Maro's catches![17]

The appearance of the Swiss poet Salomon Gessner's first collection of German prose idylls in 1756 marked the beginning of a short but interesting revival of Theocritean pastoral, of little intrinsic merit but of some importance as a preparation for the growth of European Romanticism.[18] Gessner knew no Greek but was apparently introduced to the *Idylls* by his more learned friend Karl Wilhelm Ramler.[19] Gessner's admirers were wont to compare his idylls with the pastoral poetry of Theocritus. This was certainly a case of comparing great things with small; since, as Herder pointed out, Gessner's *Idyllen* hardly measured up to the *Idylls* of Theocritus, which had "originality and passion, the two essentials of poetry, that are completely lacking in the poetry of Gessner."[20]

But the European vogue of Gessner's *Idyllen*, made possible primarily by the French translation (*Idylles de M. Gessner*, 1762) with its preface by Turgot, the future finance minister of Louis XVI, stimulated new interest in Theocritus as well. A spate of German translations of Theocritus in the second half of the eighteenth century bore witness to the desire of a large and Greekless reading audience to discover Gessner's illustrious classical model. Until that time, Germans had read Theocritus only in small numbers. With the translations of Lieberkeuhn (1757), Schwabe (1770), and von Finckenstein (1789), Theocritus was put in the hands of Gessner's many Greekless but enthusiastic readers. Eventually a major German poet, Eduard Mörike, was to undertake a partial translation of the *Idylls* (*Idyllen des Theokrit*, 1855—a translation of *Idylls I - VI, X, XI, XV, XVI*, and *XXVIII*); the result was predictably the best of all modern translations of Theocritus.

André Chénier, Chateaubriand, and Leopardi shared the late eighteenth century's love for the *Idylls*,[21] but perhaps the most interesting instance of Theocritus' influence on European literature thanks to the vogue of Gessner was to occur in Russia.[22] Pushkin credited Anton Delvig with "making the delicate roses of Theocritus bloom in the Russian snow," but it was actually Delvig's friend Nikolay Ivanovich Gnedich (1784 - 1833) who was most inspired by the Greek poet. Gnedich knew Greek well, and had genuine talent as a poet; his translation of *Idyll XV* ("The Syracusan Women") is still famous. He had been blind in one eye since childhood—a fact which perhaps accounts for some of his interest in the one-eyed Cyclops of *Idyll XI*. The immediate literary stimulus for his humorous version of *Idyll XI* ("The Cyclops" 1813) was the earlier version (1807) of Merzlyakov, which mixed Russian folk verse and popular expressions rather incongruously with the thoroughly Greek subject matter of Theocritus' original poem. Gnedich decided that the total transposition of the material was called for, and presented in his Russian eclogue a Cyclops who sings of Galatea from a window of his home in St. Petersburg! This parodic use of Theocritean material prepared Gnedich for the task of responding with greater originality to the spirit of the *Idylls*. In the foreword to translation of *Idyll XV* (1820 - 1821), he urged a return to Theocritus as a model for the idyll; but what interested him most was not the pastoralism but the vivid realism of the *Idylls* and their evocation of scenes from the daily lives of ordinary people. Gnedich was the first to follow his own literary advice, and published in 1821 a memorable Russian idyll, "The Fishermen" *(Rybaki)*, inspired by *Idyll XV* as well as by the pseudo-Theocritean *Idyll XXI*.

From the beginning of the nineteenth century to our own time a growing number of editions and translations of Theocritus (including translations into Catalan, Czech, Hungarian, Modern Greek, Polish, Russian, and Swedish) have made the poet's works available to what is probably a larger number of readers than at any time in history. Yet little direct influence of Theocritus is to be found in the significant poetry of the times. No doubt, two masterpieces of English Romanticism, Shelley's "Adonais" and Arnold's "Thyrsis," are pastoral elegies which derive ultimately from Theocritean models.[23] However, an unexpected and strikingly original recreation of the pastoral monologue as exemplified by *Idyll XI* can be found in "The Afternoon of a Faun" *(L'Après-midi d'un faune*, 1876) of the French poet Stéphane Mallarmé; my article "Mallarmé's Symbolist Eclogue: The 'Faune' as Pastoral" deals with its relationship to the themes and motifs of the Theocritean tradition.[24]

IV Theocritus Today

Theocritus has yet to find his ideal American (or English) translator. Writing to his mother on the subject of his recently composed pastoral elegy "Thyrsis" Matthew Arnold remarked that "the diction of the poem was modelled on that of Theocritus, whom I have been much reading during the two years this poem has been forming itself. . . . I meant the diction to be *so artless as to be almost heedless*" (my italics).[25] This may not be a completely satisfying definition of the problem of finding an adequate English equivalent of Theocritus' Greek pastoral style, but it makes one regret that Arnold never did for Theocritus in England what Morike had done for him in Germany. Of course, there is nothing more taxing than to make artfulness appear "heedless" and "artless," yet this is just what Theocritus' learned amalgam of dialects succeeds in doing in the pastoral poems and mimes.

The best of the recent translations (the one by Barriss Mills) is thoroughly colorless in its style—a virtue, in that at least it can be said to avoid *false* color—and maintains an even if modest level of poetic resonance. What remains to be attempted, in my opinion, is a vividly alert translation of the *Pastoral Idylls* and mimes into a nonstandard literary English which could combine some of the charm of the dialects used in *Huckleberry Finn* with a light touch of archaism of the sort found in *The Sot-Weed Factor*. I doubt very much, however, if Robert Frost's New England pastoral idiom would be a good model; I can imagine Theocritus' herdsmen as hillbillies, but not as Yankees.

The *Pastoral Idylls* and mimes of Theocritus are semidramatic in their radical of presentation. Since it is unlikely that any translator will be able to do full justice to the poetic merit of the best of Theocritus' verse, other means of communicating its charm and fascination should not be neglected. A staged English version of "The Syracusan Women" *(Idyll XV)* would, I believe, easily meet with applause. But the other mimes, as well as the entire sequence of the *Pastoral Idylls,* might also go over well with modern theater audiences, especially if music of the appropriate sort (Country Western? Andean flute music?) and pantomime (the death of Daphnis in *Idyll I,* for example) were to enhance the production. I personally look forward to the time when some enterprising theater company will dare to invite audiences to an evening of Theocritean mime.

Aristocratic versions of pastoral, from the Renaissance onwards, rarely if ever took the Theocritean Herdsman-Poet equation at face value; shepherds' robes were only, as Raymond Williams has pointed out, "the fancy dress of court games."[26] Once the figure of the shepherd-courtier faded away at the end of the eighteenth century, the Theocritean Herdsman-Poet equation vanished almost completely from European poetry. Wordsworth's shepherds or country people are not truly joined with the poet in universal brotherhood: *he* is a poet, *they* are herdsmen, and never the twain shall meet. But it is possible that in modern democratic America, whose Mark Twains have been roughing it for generations, a more

Theocritean form of Pastoral could take new birth, free of the taint of educated condescension or elitist pride, in which the figure of the poet who earns his living taking care of livestock would resurrect old myths of human freedom and universal brotherhood.

Finally, the Theocritean perspective on eros and creativity challenges a number of modern cultural assumptions.[27] The singing Theocritean Herdsman may seem a hopelessly Utopian figure to modern Western man who, having resigned himself to a radical division between working hours and leisure time, can barely imagine a life where work and creative play would be constantly joined together; and who, having sacrificed his dreams of happiness to the greater efficiency of the economic system, only desires to have his work rewarded with the highest possible salary and his leisure time devoted to the greatest possible accumulation of sense pleasures. By way of contrast, the Theocritean Herdsman-Poet transforms work (the herdsman's tasks) into play (the poet's song), and devotes his most idle hours to the freely chosen sublimation of eros (the love for Amaryllis, Galatea, etc.) in the direction of song, the symbol of the liberating activation of the creative impulse throughout the *Pastoral Idylls*. Whether this imagined reconciliation of the pleasure principle with the reality principle is only a dream, or whether the idyllic vision provides us with a glimpse of a new era of human freedom, is not the least of the questions Theocritus might inspire us to ask.

Notes and References

Chapter One

1. For a discussion of the external and internal evidence relating to the life of Theocritus and the dating of his works, see *Theocritus*, ed. and trans. A. S. F. Gow (Cambridge, 1952), I, pp. xv - xxix; hereafter cited as Gow.

2. See especially P. M. Fraser, *Ptolemaic Alexandria* (Oxford, 1972) and F. E. Peters, *The Harvest of Hellenism* (New York, 1970). The standard introduction continues to be W. W. Tarn, *Hellenistic Civilization* (London, 1930).

3. For the history of Syracuse and Sicily, see M. I. Finley, *Ancient Sicily* (New York, 1968).

4. Richmond Y. Hathorn, "The Ritual Origin of Pastoral," *Transactions of the American Philological Association* XCII (1961): 235 - 37.

5. Paul MacKendrick, *The Greek Stones Speak* (New York, 1962), pp. 346 - 49. See also C. Kerenyi, *Asklepios* (New York, 1959), pp. 47 - 69.

6. Alice Lindsell, "Was Theocritus a Botanist?" *Greece and Rome* VI: 17 (1937): 78.

7. Ibid., p. 83 ff.

8. Richard Reitzenstein, *Epigramm und Skolion* (Giessen, 1893), pp. 193 - 263.

9. For the ancient "life" of Diogenes, see *Diogenes Laertius: Lives of Eminent Philosophers*, trans. R. D. Hicks (Cambridge, Mass., 1925), II, pp. 22 - 81. See also M. I. Finley's entertaining essay in *Aspects of Antiquity* (New York, 1969), pp. 89 - 101.

10. Thomas G. Rosenmeyer, *The Green Cabinet: Theocritus and the European Pastoral Lyric* (Berkeley, Calif., 1969), pp. 10 - 11 and passim. Rosenmeyer's exploration of this topic prompted my own investigations. For a systematic presentation of the ideas of Epicurus regarding happiness and friendship, see George A. Panichas, *Epicurus* (New York, 1967), especially pp. 98 - 122. Most of the extant remains of Epicurus are to be found in the tenth book of Diogenes Laertius, but see also *Epicurus: The Extant Remains*, ed. and trans. Cyril Bailey (Oxford, 1926).

11. *Diogenes Laertius*, X.148.

12. Ibid., X.118.

13. Ibid.

14. Epicurus also used the term (*hēsuchia* in Attic Greek) at least once: see *Principle Doctrines* XIV in Bailey's edition.

151

15. See the monumental study of P. M. Fraser, *Ptolemaic Alexandria*.
16. Ibid., Vol. I, p. 70.
17. Ibid., pp. 117 - 18.
18. Ibid., pp. 312 - 35.
19. Ibid., pp. 307, 314.
20. C. P. *Cavafy: Collected Poems*, trans. Edmund Keeley and Philip Sherrard (Princeton, 1975), p. 34.
21. *Plutarch's Moralia*, trans. Phillip H. De Lacy and Benedict Einarson (Cambridge, Mass., 1959), 601F.
22. See Terry Eagleton, *Marxism and Literary Criticism* (Berkeley, Calif., 1976), pp. 34 - 36.
23. For the term "counterforce," see Leo Marx, *The Machine in the Garden* (Oxford, 1964), pp. 25 - 26. The actual "counterforce" in the *Pastoral Idylls* is not so much political (although there is certainly a *latent* social and political dimension to the poems, which I have touched on here) as psychological: sexual passion is the force which threatens—and in Daphnis' case, destroys—the idyllic life of Theocritus' herdsmen-poets.

Chapter Two

1. Gilbert Lawall, *Theocritus; Coan Pastorals: A Poetry Book* (Cambridge, Mass., 1967), hereafter cited as Lawall. Cf. Charles Segal in *Classical Review* LXIII: 5 (1968): 228: "The least convincing part of Lawall's book is the thesis that Idylls 1 - 7 form a unified collection of Coan poems."
2. Charles Segal, "Death by Water: A Narrative Pattern in Theocritus (Idylls 1, 13, 22, 23)," *Hermes* 102 (1974): 21 - 22.
3. See Charles Segal, " 'Since Daphnis Dies,' " *Museum Helveticum* 31 (1974): 3.
4. Compare Milton's imitation of this passage in "Lycidas," ll. 50 ff.: "Where were ye Nymphs when the remorseless deep/Clos'd o're the head of your lov'd *Lycidas?*" etc.
5. See the note on *Idyll I* l. 85 in *Theocritus: Select Poems*, ed. K. J. Dover (London, 1971); hereafter cited as Dover.
6. See in particular: R. M. Ogilvie, "The Song of Thyrsis," *Journal of Hellenic Studies* 82 (1962): 106 - 10; Ernst A. Schmidt, "Die Leiden des verliebten Daphnis," *Hermes* 96 (1968): 539 - 52; F. J. Williams, "Theocritus, *Idyll* i 81 - 91," *Journal of Hellenic Studies* LXXXIX (1969): 121 - 23; and Charles Segal, " 'Since Daphnis Dies': The Meaning of Theocritus' First Idyll," *Museum Helveticum* 31 (1974): 1 - 22.
7. Segal, " 'Since Daphnis Dies,' " p. 12.
8. Thus Lawall sees Daphnis as a hero of chastity: "Both Hippolytus and Daphnis wish to preserve their purity at all costs, even that of death" (*Coan Pastorals*, p. 19). Later, in a footnote (p. 127), he says, "Theocritus' version must rather be accepted on its own terms." I agree, and feel that

the Euripidean Hippolytus constitutes a misleading analogy.

9. See Gow's note on *Idyll* VII.92 for the Nymphs = Muses equation or near equation; Gow does not quite accept it.

10. Williams, "Idyll i 81 - 91," 123. In *Idyll XIII* ll. 43 - 44 Theocritus also describes Nymphs *dancing*.

11. *Symposium* 209.

12. An enterprising lover might even bring torches and axes to burn and smash his way into his beloved's house, as in *Idyll II* l. 128. Cf. Otis Redding's song "Open the Door," which offers exact parallels with the Greek *paraklausithyron* with its refrain "let me in" and the threat "open the door, or I'll bust it in."

13. Theocritus mentions just such a cave in *Idyll VII* ll. 136 - 37.

14. Dover's note on *Idyll III* l. 9.

15. Lawall, p. 56.

16. See Chapter 3, section IV of this book for a discussion of Greek paederasty.

17. Gavin Maxwell, *The Ten Pains of Death* (New York, 1960), p. 49.

18. Ibid., p. 50.

19. Ibid., p. 51.

20. John B. Van Sickle, "Poetica teocritea," *Quaderni Urbinati di cultura classica* IX (1970): 80.

21. Lawall, pp. 59 - 60.

22. See Dover's note on *Idyll V* ll. 148 f.

23. See Gow's preface to *Idyll VI*, pp. 118 - 19 (Vol. II).

24. Ibid., pp. 119 - 20.

25. Lawall, p. 70.

26. C. G. Jung, *Aion: Researches into the Phenomenology of the Self*, 2nd ed., trans. R. F. C. Hull (Princeton, 1959), p. 13.

27. For bibliography and introduction to the main lines of interpretation, see Charles Segal, "Theocritus' Seventh Idyll and Lycidas," *Wiener Studien* Neue Folge 8 (87) (1974): 20 - 76.

28. Lawall, pp. 80 - 82.

29. See the discussion of symposiastic themes in Chapter 3, section I of this book.

30. John H. Finley, Jr., *Four Stages of Greek Thought* (Stanford, 1966), p. 107.

31. See, for example, Erling B. Holtsmark, "Poetry as Self-Enlightenment: Theocritus 11," *Transactions of the American Philological Association* XCVII (1966): 253 - 59. See also the earlier appreciation of the medical metaphor by Victor Magnien, "La médecine et la philosophie dans le "Cyclope" de Théocrite," *Acropole* II (1927): 97 - 111.

32. See Gow's preface to *Idyll XI*, p. 209 (Vol. II).

33. *Diogenes Laertius* X.118.

34. See Chapter 5, section I for a discussion of Virgil's use of these motifs. The single most famous example in English is Christopher

Marlowe's "The Passionate Shepherd to His Love" with its listing of the present which the lover offers in order to persuade his beloved to "come live with me and be my love."

35. In *Idyll I* it was also the *frame* which dramatized the theme of friendship.

36. See Gow's discussion of the manuscript tradition, pp. xxx - lix (Vol. I).

37. Lawall, p. 3.

38. Ibid., p. 115.

39. See Charles Segal, "Thematic Coherence and Levels of Style in Theocritus' Bucolic Idylls," *Wiener Studien* (1977): 35 - 68, for a brilliant argument in favor of this position.

Chapter Three

1. See Gow's note on *Idyll X* l. 26.

2. Francis Cairns, *Generic Composition in Greek and Roman Poetry* (Edinburgh, 1972), p. 75; hereafter cited as Cairns.

3. Ibid., p. 76.

4. Francis Cairns, "Theocritus Idyll 10," *Hermes* 98 (1970): 40.

5. See Cairns, p. 169 ff.

6. *Matthew Arnold: Lectures and Essays in Criticism,* ed. R. H. Super (Ann Arbor, 1962), p. 216.

7. Ibid., p. 220.

8. Ibid., p. 222.

9. Ibid.

10. Gow, p. 265 (Vol. II).

11. Erich Neumann, *The Origins and History of Consciousness,* trans. R. F. C. Hull (Princeton, 1954), pp. 78, 97, 224 n.8.

12. *C. G. Jung: Letters 1951 - 1961,* ed. Gerhard Adler and Aniela Jaffé, trans. R. F. C. Hull (Princeton, 1975), p. 244. Jung wrote this letter in English.

13. Dover, pp. 209 - 10.

14. *Arnold: Lectures and Essays,* p. 222.

15. Marcel Detienne, *Les jardins d'Adonis* (Paris, 1972), pp. 159 - 72. See, for the reference as well as a résumé of Detienne's remarks, Charles Segal, "Simaetha and the Iynx (Theocritus, Idyll II)," *Quaderni Urbinati di cultura classica* XV (1973): 32 - 35.

16. Neumann, *The Origins and History of Consciousness,* pp. 57 - 58.

17. Alfred Koerte, *Hellenistic Poetry,* trans. Jacob Hammer and Moses Hadas (New York, 1929), p. 319.

18. Segal, "Simaetha and the Iynx," p. 41.

19. Dover, p. 253.

20. Gow, p. 415 (Vol. II).

21. G. Karl Galinsky, *The Herakles Theme: The Adaptations of the Hero in Literature from Homer to the Twentieth Century* (Totowa, N.J., 1972), p. 117.

22. See the chapter "From Homer to Virgil: The Obsolescence of Epic" in Brooks Otis, *Virgil: A Study in Civilized Poetry* (Oxford, 1964), pp. 5 - 40, especially pp. 8 - 15.

23. Quoted in Robert Thomas Kerlin, *Theocritus in English Literature* (Lynchburg, Va., 1910), p. 114.

24. Donald J. Mastronarde, "Theocritus Idyll 13: Love and the Hero," *Transactions of the American Philological Association* 99 (1968): 280 - 81.

25. Segal, "Death by Water," p. 28.

26. T. B. L. Webster, *Hellenistic Poetry and Art* (London, 1964), p. 86.

27. Gow, p. 383 (Vol. II).

28. *The Greek Bucolic Poets*, trans. J. M. Edmonds (Cambridge, Mass., 1928), pp. xvi - xvii (Introduction).

29. Ibid., p. xxi.

30. See his essay "The Idylls of Theocritus" (1842).

31. Gow, p. 305 (Vol. II).

32. Norman Austin, "Theocritus and Simonides," *Transactions of the American Philological Association* 98 (1967): 11.

33. Cairns, p. 110.

34. George Devereux, "Greek Pseudo-Homosexuality and the 'Greek Miracle,' " *Symbolae Osloenses* XLII (1967): 82.

35. Dover, p. 104. See also K. J. Dover, "Eros and Nomos (Plato, *Symposium* 182A - 185C)," *University of London, Institute of Classical Studies Bulletin* XI (1964): 31 - 42. The articles by Dover and Devereux are the most enlightening studies of Greek paederasty available in English; they inspired the present discussion of the topic. See now also Dover's *Greek Homosexuality* (Cambridge, Mass., 1978).

36. Dover, "Eros and Nomos," p. 39.

37. Devereux, "Greek Pseudo-Homosexuality," p. 78.

38. Ibid., pp. 77 - 78.

39. Webster, *Hellenistic Poetry and Art*, p. 86.

40. See Gow, p. 221 (Vol. II).

41. Giuseppe Giangrande, "Theocritus' Twelfth and Fourth Idylls: A Study in Hellenistic Irony," *Quaderni Urbinati di cultura classica* XII (1971): 95 - 113.

42. Ibid., 101 - 105.

43. Cairns, p. 25.

44. Ibid., p. 30 - 31.

45. Dover, "Eros and Nomos," p. 31.

46. Ibid., p. 39.

47. Cairns, pp. 84 - 85.

Chapter Four

1. Gow's note on *Idyll XI* l. 18.
2. See Thomas G. Rosenmeyer, *The Green Cabinet: Theocritus and the European Pastoral Lyric* (Berkeley, Calif., 1969), pp. 32 - 33 and footnotes 9 - 11.
3. See Ulrich Ott, "Theokrits Thalysien und ihre litterarischen Vorbilder," *Rheinisches Museum* 115 (1972): 134 - 49. See also, for a brief account, Segal, "Theocritus' Seventh Idyll and Lycidas," pp. 22 - 23.
4. Dover, p. lxiii.
5. George Soutar, *Nature in Greek Poetry* (London, 1939), pp. 111 - 12.
6. Clyde Murley, "Plato's 'Phaedrus' and Theocritean Pastoral," *Transactions of the American Philological Association* LXXI (1940): 282.
7. Rosenmeyer, *The Green Cabinet*, pp. 41 - 42.
8. For a complete introduction to Herondas, see Frederic Will, *Herondas* (New York, 1973).
9. David Craig, "Towards the Laws of Literary Development," in *Marxists on Literature: An Anthology*, ed. David Craig (Baltimore, 1975), p. 160.
10. In the Metropolitan Museum of Art, see the astonishing statue of an old peasant woman going to market.
11. Northrop Frye, *Anatomy of Criticism* (New York, 1968), p. 285.
12. *Herodas: Mimiambi*, ed. I. C. Cunningham (Oxford, 1971), p. 14.
13. Frye, *Anatomy of Criticism*, p. 42.
14. For a discussion of Asclepiades, see Fraser, *Ptolemaic Alexandria*, I, pp. 562 - 67.
15. Ibid., pp. 717 - 92, for an excellent presentation of Callimachus.
16. T. B. L. Webster, *The Age of Hellenism* (New York, 1966), p. 64.
17. Ellen Frye, *The Marble Threshing Floor: A Collection of Greek Folksongs* (Austin, Texas, 1973), p. 217.
18. Gow, p. 35 (Vol. II).
19. Ibid., pp. 231 - 32, 382 - 84.
20. Webster, *Hellenistic Poetry*, pp. 65 - 66.
21. Dover, p. 181. For a discussion of Theocritus as a critic of Apollonius, see Otis, *Virgil*, pp. 398 - 405.
22. Webster, *The Age of Hellenism*, pp. 64 - 72; *Hellenistic Poetry*, pp. 163 - 66.
23. Webster, Hellenistic Poetry, 165 - 66; Lawall, pp. 80 - 82 (Lycidas as satyr) and frontispiece.
24. Margarete Bieber, *The Sculpture of the Hellenistic Age* (New York, 1961), pp. 136 - 56.
25. Dryden's *Dedication of Virgil's . Pastorals*, quoted in Kernin, *Theocritus in English Literature*, p. 21.
26. Gow, p. lxxiii (Vol. I).

27. Dover, p. xxxix.

28. See Ph.-E Legrand, *La Poésie Alexandrine* (Paris, 1924), pp. 133 - 37.

Chapter Five

1. For an excellent study and bilingual anthology of the European pastoral elegy, see Thomas Perrin Harrison, Jr., *The Pastoral Elegy: An Anthology* (Austin, Texas, 1939). For a full presentation of "Lycidas" as a pastoral elegy, see Scott Elledge, *Milton's "Lycidas"* (New York, 1966).

2. For a sensitive study of *Daphnis and Chloe*, see William E. McCulloh, *Longus* (New York, 1970).

3. A. Cartault, *Étude sur les Bucoliques de Virgile* (Paris, 1897), pp. 102 - 03.

4. See, in Ida Maïer, *Ange Politien* (Geneva, 1966), the chapter "La 'contaminatio,' constante de l'art d'écrire."

5. See Leo Marx, *The Machine in the Garden* (Oxford, 1964), pp. 25 - 26.

6. Otis, *Virgil*, p. 136.

7. Ernst Robert Curtius, *European Literature and the Latin Middle Ages*, trans. Willard R. Trask (New York, 1953), p. 190.

8. See my article " 'Poetry is/is not a cure for love:' the Conflict of Theocritean and Petrarchan *Topoi* in the *Shepheardes Calender*," *Studies in Philology*, LXXVI, 4 (Fall, 1979), 353 - 365.

9. Jean Seznec, *The Survival of the Pagan Gods*, trans. Barbara F. Sessions (New York, 1953), p. 163.

10. *Petrarch's Bucolicum Carmen*, trans. Thomas G. Bergin (New Haven, 1974), p. 157.

11. Ibid., Bergin's note on X ll. 164 - 65, p. 241.

12. R. R. Bolgar, *The Classical Heritage* (Cambridge, 1954), p. 279.

13. Alice Hulubéi, *L'Églogue en France au XVIe siècle* (Paris, 1938), p. 42.

14. Henry Fielding, *Joseph Andrews* (New York, 1950), p. 94 (Book Two, Chapter II).

15. Preface to *The Shepherd's Week*.

16. *The Beauties of English Poetry* (c. 1765). Quoted in Kerlin, *Theocritus in English Literature*, p. 77.

17. Ibid., p. 81.

18. See Paul Van Tieghem, *Le Préromantisme* (Paris, 1948), Vol. II, pp. 207 - 311, "Les Idylles de Gessner et le rêve pastoral."

19. John Hibberd, *Salomon Gessner* (Cambridge, 1976), pp. 27 - 28.

20. *Fragments Concerning Recent German Literature* (1766 - 1767).

21. See Stephen Rogers, *Classical Greece and the Poetry of Chénier, Shelley, and Leopardi* (Notre Dame, Ind., 1974).

22. In this paragraph, I follow the research of Mara Kazoknieks, *Stu-*

dien zur Rezeption der Antike bei Russischen Dichtern zu Beginn des XIX. Jahrhunderts (Munich, 1968).

23.   See the presentation and analysis of "Adonais" and "Thyrsis" in Harrison, *The Pastoral Elegy*.

24.   Steven F. Walker, "Mallarmé's Symbolist Eclogue: the 'Faune' as Pastoral," *PMLA (Publications of the Modern Language Association)* 93: 1 (January, 1978): 106 - 17.

25.   Quoted in Harrison, *The Pastoral Elegy*, p. 22.

26.   Raymond Williams, *The Country and the City* (New York, 1973), p. 21.

27.   Remarks inspired by Herbert Marcuse, *Eros and Civilization: A Philosophical Inquiry into Freud* (New York, 1955).

Selected Bibliography

(This bibliography lists only those books and articles which, in my opinion, are most likely to prove useful to the nonspecialist. Preference has been given to recent scholarship in English.)

PRIMARY SOURCES

1. Texts, translations, and commentaries

DOVER, K. J. *Theocritus: Select Poems*. London: Macmillan, 1971. Greek text of the major poems, with excellent introduction and commentary. Greek-English vocabulary. The best school edition.

EDMONDS, J. M. *The Greek Bucolic Poets* (Loeb ed.). Cambridge, Mass.: Harvard University Press; London: William Heinemann, 1970. Reprint of revised 1928 edition. Introduction, Greek text with facing English prose translation, and index. Useful, but largely superseded by Gow's edition. Includes other Hellenistic bucolic poems.

FRITZ, F. P. *Theokrit: Gedichte*. Tübingen: Heimeran Verlag, 1970. The major poems, with Greek text and facing German translation. Good commentary.

GOW, A. S. F. *Bucolici Graeci*. Oxford: Clarendon Press, 1952. (Reprinted several times.) Greek text and apparatus only. The average Hellenist will require an edition with commentary.

_____. *The Greek Bucolic Poets*. Hamden, Conn.: Archon Books, 1972. Reprint of the 1953 Cambridge University Press edition. English prose translation, brief notes and introduction. The "small Gow" for the Greekless reader. Includes translations of other Hellenistic bucolic poems as well.

_____. *Theocritus*. Cambridge: Cambridge University Press, 1952 (two volumes). The first volume contains the introduction, Greek text and facing prose translations of the complete works of Theocritus as well as *pseudo-Theocritea*. The second volume contains Gow's monumental commentary, a bibliography, an index and plates. Beyond praise. Completely fulfills the aim of an edition cum translation and commentary, which is to make a difficult text thoroughly accessible.

HOLDEN, ANTHONY. *Greek Pastoral Poetry*. Baltimore: Penguin Books, 1973. Introduction, readable translations in prosaic verse, brief notes, glossary.

MILLS, BARRISS. *The Idylls of Theokritos*. West Lafayette, Ind.: Purdue University Studies, 1963. The best translation of Theocritus into

English. A beautiful book, well printed and tastefully illustrated. Useless introductory essay.

MÖRIKE, EDUARD. *Idyllen des Theokrit*. [1855] A major Greek poet translated by a major German poet. Translations of *Idylls* I - VI, X, XI, XV, XVI, and XXVIII—unfortunately, Mörike never got around to *Idyll* VII.

RIST, ANNA. *The Poems of Theocritus*. Chapel Hill: University of North Carolina Press, 1978. Translation with commentaries.

SECONDARY SOURCES

1. The *Idylls*: Scholarship and Criticism

ARNOLD, MATTHEW. "Pagan and Mediaeval Religious Sentiment," in *Matthew Arnold: Lectures and Essays in Criticism*, ed. R. H. Super. Ann Arbor: University of Michigan Press, 1962 (pp. 212 - 31). Includes a lively and polemical discussion of *Idyll* XV ("The Syracusan Women"). Arnold at his best.

AUSTIN, NORMAN. "Theocritus and Simonides," *Transactions of the American Philological Association* 98 (1967): 1 - 21. Emphasizes the tensions and contradictions which make *Idyll* XVI ("The Graces") an interesting poem.

CAIRNS, FRANCIS. *Generic Composition in Greek and Roman Poetry*. Edinburgh: Edinburgh University Press, 1972. Ingenious analyses of a number of Theocritus' poems from a classical generic perspective.

EDQUIST, HARRIET. "Aspects of Theocritean Otium," *Ramus* 4:2 (1975): 101 - 14. The theme of *hasychia* in the pastoral poems, especially *Idylls* I and VII. The article forms part of a special volume of *Ramus* on ancient pastoral (ed. A. J. Boyle) which deserves attention.

FABIANO, GIANFRANCO. "Fluctuation in Theocritus' Style," *Greek, Roman and Byzantine Studies* 12:4 (1971): 517 - 37. Linguistic and literary analysis of the variety of styles found in the *Idylls*.

GIANGRANDE, GIUSEPPE. "Theocritus' Twelfth and Fourth Idylls: A Study in Hellenistic Irony," *Quaderni Urbinati di cultura classica* 12 (1971): 95 - 113. The technique followed by Theocritus to achieve ironic effects in two of his poems.

HOLTSMARK, ERLING B. "Poetry as Self-Enlightenment: Theocritus 11," *Transactions of the American Philological Association* 97 (1966): 253 - 59. Discussion of the motivating idea of *Idyll* XI ('poetry is the cure for love').

LAWALL, GILBERT. *Theocritus' Coan Pastorals: A Poetry Book*. Cambridge, Mass.: Harvard University Press, 1967. Epoch-making study of *Idylls* I - VII as a bucolic collection.

LEGRAND, PH. E. *Étude sur Théocrite*. [1898] Paris: E. de Boccard, 1968. A classic study, dated but still interesting.

LINDSELL, ALICE. "Was Theocritus a Botanist?" *Greece and Rome* 6:17 (1937): 78 - 93. Entertaining piece of scholarly detective work.

MAGNIEN, VICTOR. "La médecine et la philosophie dans le 'Cyclope' de Théocrite," *Acropole* 2 (1927): 97 - 111. Discussion of the idea of a cure for love in *Idyll* XI in relation to Greek medicine.

MASTRONARDE, DONALD J. "Theocritus Idyll 13: Love and the Hero," *Transactions of the American Philological Association* 99 (1968): 273 - 90. A sensitive reading of *Idyll* XIII ("Hylas"): "the hero cannot remain heroic in love."

MURLEY, CLYDE. "Plato's 'Phaedrus' and Theocritean Pastoral," *Transactions of the American Philological Association* 71 (1940): 281 - 95. Pioneering study of what Plato shared with Theocritus.

OTT, ULRICH. *Die Kunst des Gegensatzes in Theokrits Hirtengedichten.* Hildesheim: Georg Olms Verlag, 1969. An analysis of *Idylls* I, III - VII, X, and XI in terms of structural contrasts. Excellent bibliographical references to German Theocritean scholarship.

SEGAL, CHARLES. "Death by Water: A Narrative Pattern in Theocritus (Idylls 1, 13, 22, 23)," *Hermes* 102 (1974): 20 - 38.

———. "Simaetha and the Iynx (Theocritus, Idyll II)," *Quaderni Urbinati di cultura classica* 15 (1973): 32 - 43.

———. " 'Since Daphnis Dies': The Meaning of Theocritus' First Idyll," *Museum Helveticum* 31 (1974): 1 - 22.

———. "Theocritean Criticism and the Interpretation of the Fourth Idyll," *Ramus* 1 (1972): 1 - 25.

———. "Thematic Coherence and Levels of Style in Theocritus' Bucolic Idylls," *Wiener Studien* (1977): 35 - 68.

———. "Theocritus' Seventh Idyll and Lycidas," *Wiener Studien* 8:87 (1974): 20 - 76. Charles Segal has produced a series of fine articles on Theocritus whose wealth of critical observations and sophisticated methodology make it the standard by which modern Theocritean scholarship may be judged. Highly recommended.

WILLIAMS, F. J. "Theocritus, *Idyll* i 81 - 91," *Journal of Hellenic Studies* 89 (1969): 121 - 23. Interesting attempt to relate the story of Daphnis in *Idyll* I to the traditional Sicilian myth.

2. Cultural and Historical Background

DEVEREUX, GEORGE. "Greek Pseudo-Homosexuality and the 'Greek Miracle,' " *Symbolae Osloenses* 42 (1967): 69 - 92. This and Dover's article (see below) are excellent discussions of Greek paederasty.

DOVER, K. J. "Eros and Nomos (Plato, *Symposium* 182A - 185C)," *University of London, Institute of Classical Studies Bulletin* 11 (1964): 31 - 42 (see above).

PETERS, F. E. *The Harvest of Hellenism: A History of the Near East from Alexander the Great to the Triumph of Christianity.* New York: Simon and Schuster, 1970. Up-to-date reference work.

POMEROY, SARAH B. *Goddesses, Whores, Wives, and Slaves: Women in Classical Antiquity.* New York: Schocken Books, 1975. Chapter VII, "Hellenistic Women," gives the cultural background information necessary for the understanding of Theocritus' treatment of women in *Idylls* II and XV.

TARN, W. W. *Hellenistic Civilisation,* third edition revised by the author and G. T. Griffith. New York: Meridian Books, 1952. A standard introduction.

TOYNBEE, ARNOLD J. *Hellenism: the History of a Civilization.* New York and London: Oxford University Press, 1959. See Chapters VIII ("Macedon's Reception of Hellenism and Opening Up of the East") and IX ("The Emancipation of Individuals from City-States").

TRYPANIS, C. A. "The Character of Alexandrian Poetry," *Greece and Rome* 16:46 (January, 1947): 1 - 7. Short introduction to the topic.

WEBSTER, T. B. L. *Hellenistic Poetry and Art.* New York: Barnes and Noble, 1964. A standard survey.

3. The *Idylls* and the Later Pastoral Tradition

BARDON, H. "Bucolique et Politique," *Rheinisches Museum* 115:2 (1972): 1 - 13. The tradition of mixing political allegory and pastoral stems from Virgil, not Theocritus.

BERG, WILLIAM. *Early Virgil.* London: University of London, Athlone Press, 1974. A good introduction to Virgil's book of eclogues. As a rule, commentators of Virgil tend to underestimate the achievement of Theocritus—Berg is no exception, unfortunately. Includes Latin text of the *Eclogues* with facing English translation.

ELLEDGE, SCOTT. *Milton's "Lycidas" (Edited to serve as an Introduction to Criticism).* New York and London: Harper and Row, 1966. Milton's lyric masterpiece in the light of the tradition of the pastoral elegy starting (more or less) with *Idyll I.* English translations of major pastoral elegies; commentary and background.

HARRISON, THOMAS PERRIN, JR. *The Pastoral Elegy: An Anthology.* Austin: University of Texas Press, 1939. Rich bilingual anthology of European pastoral elegies, with commentary and notes.

MARX, LEO. *The Machine in the Garden: Technology and the Pastoral Ideal in America.* Oxford: Oxford University Press, 1964. Opens a new theoretical and historical perspective on the pastoral mode. The first chapter introduces the term "counterforce."

McCULLOH, WILLIAM E. *Longus.* New York: Twayne Publishers, 1970. A sensitive study of *Daphnis and Chloe,* a Greek pastoral romance. Good discussion of the Theocritean influence.

OTIS, BROOKS. *Virgil: A Study in Civilized Poetry.* Oxford: Oxford University Press, 1964. The chapter "The Young Virgil" (pp. 98 - 143) is an excellent description of the Romanization of Theocritean pastoral in the *Eclogues.*

RosENMEYER, THOMAS G. *The Green Cabinet: Theocritus and the Euro-pean Pastoral Lyric.* Berkeley: University of California Press, 1969. A learned and impressive study of Theocritean pastoral from a generic perspective. A nondramatic conception of pastoral, with emphasis on the lyric elements and their later imitation. Makes a convincing case for considering Theocritus' *Pastoral Idylls* as *the* model for European pastoral.

VAN SICKLE, JOHN. "The Unity of the *Eclogues:* Arcadian Forest, Theocri-tean Trees," *Transactions of the American Philological Association* 98 (1967): 491 - 508. Excellent discussion of Virgil's transformation of Theocritean pastoral.

WALKER, STEVEN F. "Mallarmé's Symbolist Eclogue: the 'Faune' as Pastoral," *PMLA* 93:1 (January, 1978). "L'Après-midi d'un faune" viewed from the perspective of Theocritean pastoral.

_____. " 'Poetry is/is not a cure for love:' the Conflict of Theocritean and Petrarchan *Topoi* in the *Shepheardes Calender,*" *Studies in Philology* LXXVI, 4, (Fall, 1979), 353 - 365. The indirect influence of Theocritus on Spenser.

Index

Adonis, 25, 46–47, 90–94
Aegon, 48–53
Agathocles, 17
Alexander the Great, 14, 24–25
Amaryllis, 43–47, 48–53, 75, 79–80, 82
anima, 63–65, 76
Anyte, 127
Apelles, 18
Aphrodite, 42, 45, 70, 73, 87, 90–93, 95
Apollonius of Rhodes, 31, 103, 128–29
Aratus (friend of Theocritus), 61, 64, 68–69, 71, 72, 80, 98
Archimedes, 27
Arethusa, 15
Aristarchus, 27
Aristophanes, 62
Aristotle, 71
Arnold, Matthew, 20, 90–91, 93–94, 147
Arsinoe, 26, 90, 94, 103
Asclepiades, 45, 125
Asclepius, 18, 111
Atalanta, 45
ataraxia, 23–24
Athenaeus, 62, 91, 103, 111, 117
Athens, 21, 22, 29, 31
Austin, Norman, 104–105

Battus, 48–53, 82
Berenike, 103
Bieber, Margarete, 129
Bion, 136
Burns, Robert, 130, 145

Cairns, Francis 88–89, 106, 109
Callimachus, 31, 44, 72, 100, 125–27, 128–29
Calypso, 47, 113

catharsis, *see katharsis*
Cavafy, C.P., 28
Comatas, 53–60, 67–70, 77, 79, 80, 81–84, 104
contaminatio, 134, 137, 157n4
Corydon, 48–53, 79, 82, 137
Cos, 17–21, 65
counterforce, 32, 152n23
Courbet, Gustave, 20–21
Craig, David, 121
creative sublimation, 42–43, 53–54, 60, 67–68, 71–72, 82–84, 149
Cunningham, I.C., 123
Curtius, Ernst Robert, 140

Damoetas, 60–64, 82, 155n35
Danae, 45
Daphnis, 15, 34–43, 54, 60–64, 67, 68, 70, 73, 79–80, 81–84, 93, 126
Demeter, 15, 46, 70
Demetrius of Phalerum, 27, 29, 31
Detienne, Marcel, 95
Devereux, George, 106, 108
dialectical progression, 36–37, 81–82
Diogenes, 21–22, 30
Dionysius I, 16–17
Dionysius II, 17
Dionysos, 21, 91, 111
Dorat, Jean, 20, 143
Doric dialect, 14, 27, 95, 130–31
Dover, K.J., 47, 93–94, 99, 100, 107, 113, 129, 130, 131
Dryden, John, 130
Dürer, Albrecht, 32–33

Edmonds, J.M., 103–104
Egypt, 24–26
Endymion, 46–47, 93
Enna, 14–15
Epicharmus, 15, 112

Epicurus, 22–24, 69–70, 75–78, 110
Erasmus, 32–33
Etna, Mt., 14, 37
Euclid, 27
Euripides, 72, 96, 117

Finley, John, 69
Fraser, P.M., 26
friendship, 23, 77–78
Frye, Northrop, 123–24

Galatea, 15, 40–41, 58, 60–65, 70–78, 80, 81–84, 116, 117–18
Galinsky, G. Karl, 100
Garcilaso, 133, 141
Gay, John, 145
Gessner, Salomon, 141, 145–46
Giangrande, Giuseppe, 109
Glauke, 50, 52
Gnedich, N.I., 133, 146–47
Goldsmith, Oliver, 145
Gow, A.S.F., 47, 56, 67, 72, 87, 91, 97, 100, 103, 104, 109, 113–14, 129, 130, 142

Hades, 15, 37, 42, 50
hasychia, 24, 151n14, 69, 98, 109
Hecate, 61, 88, 118
Heracles, 15, 55, 99–101
Herdsman-Poet, myth of, 30–31
Hermes, 36–37
Herondas, 18, 31, 86, 121–24
Hesiod, 61, 88, 118
Hessus, Helius Eobanus, 141, 143
Hiero II, 17, 104–105
Hippocrates, 17
Hippolytus, 39–40
humor, 40, 44–46, 59–60, 68, 75, 87, 99, 109, 138
Hunt, Leigh, 101–102
Hylas, 55, 100–101, 127

Iasion, 46–47, 93
idyll (generic term), 85–86
Iliad, 18, 61, 103, 114, 116–17, 119–20
irony, 22, 48, 53, 68, 86, 88

Joseph Andrews, 144–45

Jung, C.G., 63–65, 76, 93

katharsis, 71, 74–75
Kennet, Basil, 85
Koerte, Alfred, 97
kōmos, 43–44, 97–98

Lacon, 53–60
Lawall, Gilbert, 34, 53, 58, 63, 66, 78, 79, 129
Legrand, Ph.-E., 131
Library, The (at Alexandria), 26–28, 113, 126
Lindsell, Alice, 18
literary allusions, art of, 113–15, 133–35
Longus, 136
Lycidas, 19–21, 57, 65–70, 77, 80, 82–83, 98, 118
Lucretius, 76

Macherey, Pierre, 32
Mallarmé, Stéphane, 133, 147
Mann, Thomas, 42
Marvell, Andrew, 135
Marx, Leo, 32
Mastronarde, Donald, 102
Maxwell, Gavin, 56
Melanthius, 59–60
Menander, 31
Milton, John, 15, 133, 152n4
mime, 120–24
Mörike, Eduard, 146, 148
Morson, 53, 57
Mozart, Wolfgang Amadeus, 50
Murley, Clyde, 120
Muses, 35, 41, 43, 54, 58–59, 62–65, 68–69, 70–71, 83–84, 88, 118
Museum, The (at Alexandria), 26–28, 44
myth, function of, 30–31, 64–65, 69, 124

Neumann, Erich, 92, 96
Nicias, 18, 70–72, 77, 78, 102, 111
Nymphs, 37, 41–43, 47, 54, 58–60, 62, 69–70, 80, 100–101, 126–27

Odysseus, 14, 17, 59, 113, 115

Odyssey, 14-15, 18, 46, 47, 59, 62, 112, 115-16
oikoumene, 28-32
Olympian Games, 48-51
Otis, Brooks, 139-40
Ovid, 62, 76-77, 99, 135

paederasty, 58, 72, 106-110
paideia, 55
Pan, 35, 54, 68
paraklausithyron, 43-45, 89, 153n12
Persephone, 15, 105
Petrarch, 142-43
Pharos, 25
Philetas, 19, 27, 66, 113, 125
Philoxenus, 16-17, 26, 62, 103, 115, 117-18
Pindar, 100, 104
plants, references to, 18-19
Plato, 16, 120
Pléiade, 20
Plutarch, 29
poetic sequence, 78-84
Poliziano, Angelo, 143
Polyphemus, 14-15, 40-41, 60-65, 70-78, 80, 81-84, 116, 117-18
Pope, Alexander, 36, 145
Praxiteles, 58
Priapus, 37-40, 42, 64, 111
Proust, Marcel, 52
Ptolemy I Soter, 25, 27, 103
Ptolemy II Philadelphus, 17, 19, 24-27, 31, 50, 90, 99, 103, 106

Raphael, 41
Reitzenstein, Richard, 21
Ronsard, Pierre de, 134-35, 144
Rosenmeyer, Thomas, 120, 151n10

Sannazaro, Jacopo, 144
Segal, Charles, 38, 97, 102
Selene, 46
sequence, *see* poetic sequence
Sicelidas, *see* Asclepiades
Sicily, 14-17
Sidney, Philip, 74
Simichidas, 19, 57, 65-71, 80, 83, 118
Simonides, 104-105
Socrates, 13
Sophron, 16, 120

Sotades, 26, 103-104
Soutar, George, 119
Spenser, Edmund, 130, 141
Stanford, W.B., 47
Stesichorus, 15, 117
sublimation, *see* creative sublimation
Symposium, 43
"symptoms of love" (generic term), 89, 96, 108
Syracuse, 14-17, 31
Syrinx, 35

Tasso, Torquato, 133
Tennyson, Alfred Lord, 100-101
Theocritus

WORKS OF:

Idyll I, 15, 23, 34-43, 54, 58, 60, 64, 73, 81-84, 93, 116, 136
Idyll II, 24, 44, 86, 95-98, 101-107
Idyll III, 43-48, 52, 63, 75, 92, 93, 133, 136
Idyll IV, 23, 48-53
Idyll V, 53-60, 63, 133
Idyll VI, 58, 60-65, 82, 134
Idyll VII, 17, 19-21, 24, 40-41, 44, 57, 61, 65-70, 73, 79, 81-84, 86, 93, 140
Idyll X, 86-89
Idyll XI, 14, 18, 24, 40-41, 61, 64, 70-78, 81-84, 88, 89, 113-115, 128, 133, 136-139, 140-41
Idyll XII, 109
Idyll XIII, 15, 24, 55, 100-102, 108, 129
Idyll XIV, 24, 32, 89-90, 95, 140
Idyll XV, 14, 18, 25-26, 29, 31, 90-95, 122-23, 136
Idyll XVI, 17, 103-106, 116
Idyll XVII, 24, 32, 99, 106
Idyll XVIII, 111
Idyll XXII, 102-103, 129
Idyll XXIV, 15, 99-100
Idyll XXVI, 111
Idyll XXVIII, 18, 110-111
Idyll XXIX, 109-110
Idyll XXX, 110-111
Epigrams, 17-18, 111-112

Theophrastus, 18

Thetis, 61
Thyrsis, 34–38, 43, 53, 82, 83
Tityrus, 67–68, 80
Tragic hero, 30
translations of Theocritus, 143–44, 146–48

Van Sickle, John, 57
Virgil, 32, 84, 125, 133, 134, 136–141, 143

Webster, T.B.L., 102, 109, 127, 129
Williams, F.J., 42
Williams, Raymond, 148
Wordsworth, William, 16, 148
women, presentation of, 94–98

Xenophon, 29
Xenea, 40, 67, 84

Zeus, 45, 46

DATE DUE

DEMCO 38-297